Making a Mosaic of Your County Fair

or

How to Put Your Entire Portfolio Into a Single Picture

A Tutorial

by Wendy Goerl

Table of Contents

Forward:
Why this book exists

My county fair and my photography journey are
inexorably intertwined. When I was in college, I worked
ticket sales at the gates, usually Gate 1, the "main gate"
located at the southwest corner of the fairgrounds. Gate 1
was a double gate that allowed two streams of cars to enter,
one coming east on Center Street, the other coming south
on Fairview Way. Pedestrians who had parked their cars
outside the fairgrounds came up an aisle between them.
Meaning no matter which direction they came from, they
had to cross a line of cars.

The other gatekeepers thought it had always been
this way, but I distinctly remembered a pedestrian gate that
must have been removed when they redid the gate area a
few years earlier. A while later we were in the fair office,
which had a number of aerial photos of previous years' fairs
on the wall, conveniently enough, taken from the
southwest. On one of them, the pedestrian gate was clearly
visible just to the north of the vehicular gates.

That event impressed upon me the ability of
photography to be an accurate record of what had been
when memories got fuzzy. Reason #1 to take pictures.

I spent most of my college years in a south-facing,
seventh-floor dorm room in Milwaukee School of
Engineering's Margaret Loock Hall. A few blocks to the
south was the "Plaza East" building, which consisted of two
towers on the northwest and southeast corners of the block
and a large atrium "tunnel" running perpendicular between
them. The towers had almost-square footprints, "almost"
because the corners facing each other had been chopped off

at 45-degree angles. The result was, I got to watch many beautiful sunsets by looking *south*, as the sun reflected off the windows of the "unsquare" side of the southeast building.

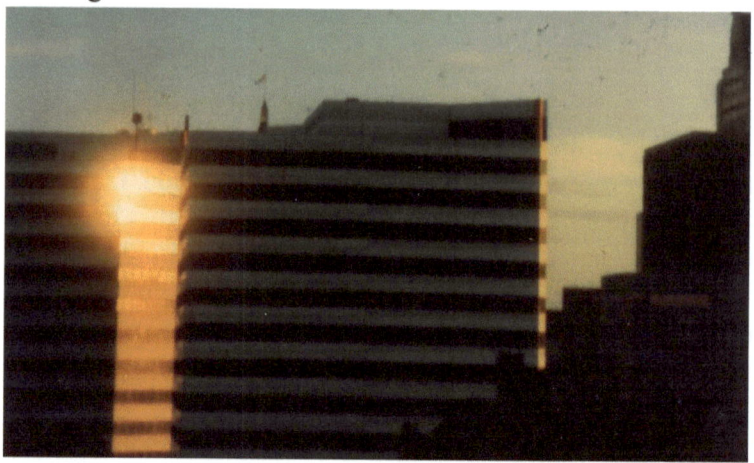

Southern sunset from my dorm room. (Regula IE 35 mm camera: probably ASA-100, probably 1/125 sec, probably f/11, 50 mm)

I loved the scene so much I tried to capture the colors, first with colored pencils and markers, then with paints. Eventually I dug out the old Regula IE, an early 1950's camera that was in an auction box my sister had won (which wasn't strange for that auction, several boxes had exactly one camera, which was unrelated to any of the other contents in the box). And the more pictures I took, the more things I found to take pictures of. Reason #2: Art.

My first job out of college was at The News, Inc., putting together a weekly newspaper. Not having any designated "reporters," whoever found a story did it. I shot four rolls and did a full-page photo essay of the fair. Reason #3: journalism.

And I've never gone to the fair without a camera since. I bought a Nikon FG and started shooting 10-20 rolls each fair, including infra-red and panoramic. I developed an interest in the nature and history of amusement rides, and realized that, while there were a fair number of books addressing roller coasters and amusement parks, there was a good deal less on the "flat" or "iron" rides of the traveling carnivals. Reason #4: I want to know the iron rides.

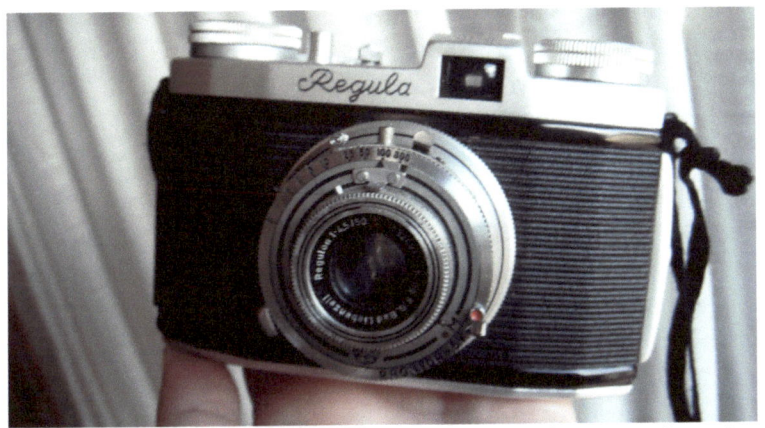

My "guessimatic" Regula IE, the camera that introduced me to 35 mm photography. Notice it's a viewfinder (the focus ring is a bit "loose," too); I have no idea if an image is properly focused or not until the film is developed. (Z70: ISO-100, 1/30 sec, F/4)

I finally bought a digital SLR for the 2011 fair and, for all the above reasons, proceeded to shoot over 1,000 photos. I put these into a mosaic that I entered the next year, hoping that, after exhibiting photography for over fifteen years, it would finally earn me a grand champion, or at least an "honorable mention."

"2011 Shawano County Fair" did win its lot, (amateur, anything goes) but in the grand and reserve, the other judge (both the amateur and professional judges judged the grand and reserve) commented that it was "just a computer program," and dismissed it in the first elimination.

The next year I entered a photo album/tutorial using 2012 photos and showing the steps (and time needed) to make a mosaic. I had fewer pictures to work with, because the memory card of a certain manufacturer (name withheld to protect the guilty) wiped itself while I was trying to upload pictures and I lost over 400 images. So if you're wondering why I don't have any cow or pig pictures, that's why. I lost all of my D60 pictures from the barns, a large portion of the midway, and over half from track-side, including the "demolition football" and trailer racing. Sure, they offered to replace the card, but they offered no help in recovering the images, and I didn't have the $250+ to send it to someplace that could attempt the recovery. I know one can't really assign a value to something as subjective as an image, but one can certainly establish a concrete value to the labor involved in recovering the images. Pity, because I had an absolutely gorgeous sunset shot of the carrousel, and the next year they replaced the incandescents with garish, bluish LED's.

But I digress. As I started to put my little photo album/tutorial into a more reproducible form, I found myself adding explanations for people who have never seen my fair, and more examples of composition and lighting challenges, until I realized I had a real book on my hands. This book.

I hope that people will read it for as many reasons as I take pictures. A time capsule of county fairs at the beginning of the new millennium. A guide to making the best photographic use of their time at the fair. A tutorial on making mosaics. And maybe even a pleasant read for its own sake.

Introduction

Why make a mosaic?

Maybe you like to take photos and want to do something new with them. Maybe you want to show off your skills, and maybe you want to get around "x number of photos" limitations. Maybe you'd just rather point pictures out than have to flip through albums, be they physical or digital. There are lots of reasons to want to create a mosaic, and while mosaic-creating programs certainly simplify the job, there's still plenty of work for you to do. Not including the work of assembling the photo library in the first place.

Why a county fair?

For myself, there are several reasons. One is I grew up within four blocks of our county's fairgrounds; I get to watch the fair set up and always spend as much time as I can at the fair. I like animals, I like amusement rides, and I can find lots of both at the fair. From a photographer's perspective, there's a huge variety of shooting situations packed into a convenient area, some of which—like the bright- and variously-lit midway at night--aren't available around small towns any other time of the year. From stop-action racing to time-lapse abstracts, from close-ups of pins to multi-frame panoramas, from daylight to sunset to natural- and artificially-lit night, you can make use of practically every mode in your camera and still have to resort to manual in many situations.

I used two digital cameras during the 2012 Fair: a Fuji Finepix Z70, which offers several shooting modes but no manual control, and a Nikon D60 single lens reflex, which I had to use in manual. The Z70 has an odd tendency to brighten reds (deep wine-colored roses consistently record as bright red) and will only center-focus and center-expose, forcing you to sometimes choose between a properly-exposed picture or a properly-focused one. But there are situations it handles better than an SLR.

With the D60 I carry a 28-70mm AF Sigma aspherical lens, a 70-210mm Quaternary lens, and a 2x Vivitar teleconverter. Some nights I take a lightweight (usually my Ambico) tripod along. Since all of these lenses are pre-digital, non-CPU[1] lenses, all of the D60 photos were taken using manual exposure. So don't ask me which mode to use! (And you'll notice a lot of "probably" in the shooting data; I have to rely on memory and experience to guess at f-stops and which lenses I was using.) I didn't carry an external flash because there are really only three situations that call for a flash: I didn't shoot in two of them and the third can be met with the built-in flash.

In Part II, the tutorial, I will be using the free version of Andrea Mosaic—a program I discovered early in my mosaic experience and which I've had no reason to switch—and a bank of 772 images created from a portion of my 2012 Shawano County Fair collection. This should be adequate to create a small 4" x 6" mosaic. If the tile size is set at ½", the program should have enough images to select from. This will result in a 152-tile mosaic. I will be taking you through the exact sequence I used to arrive at the

---

1   One day at the 2014 fair, I changed lenses from the Nikkor to the Sigma, and the D60 suddenly insisted I lock the Sigma's aperture ring at its smallest diameter (f/22). After completely ignoring the lens, metering-wise, for two years, the metering had suddenly decided to talk to it! The metering has coupled ever since. Go figure. The lens still won't autofocus, even though the D60 is the second autofocus camera it's been on.

image I did, hopefully so you won't take as many detours as I did in getting to an acceptable mosaic. And to show you that, for all the program does, you've got a fair share of work to do, too.

(And for the record, the photos in Part 1 are just as the camera shot them, with no cropping, corrections, or any post-process tweaking. They've merely been re-sized so my computer wouldn't choke trying to handle all of them in the same document.)

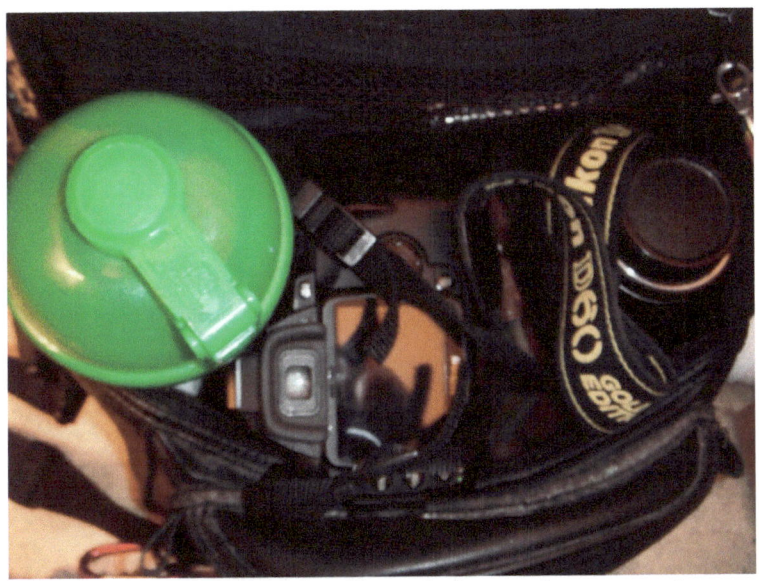

My fair-going camera kit. From left to right: souvenir cup (which has since been moved to a duct-tape holster that I snap in the front of the bag because the o-ring leaks), Nikon D60, my billfold. Nikkor E-series 70-210 (the focus ring on the Quaternary locked up in 2013, so I had to switch to the less-compact Nikkor). This was taken with the Z70, which normally rides in the exterior pocket. (Z70: ISO-800, f/4,1/4 sec, flash)

Part I: Fun at the Fair

So.

The first order of business is to acquire some images. In general a DSLR camera will have the advantage, though there are some situations that favor the small-diameter lens of a pocket camera. You're welcome to shoot film, but you're going to have to digitize the images for the mosaic program, anyway, so unless you've got some special film-only effects you're aiming for, you may as well save the time and money of developing several dozen rolls and shoot digital in the first place.

Remember, while it's theoretically possible to make a mosaic using one image and altering the value and color to whatever is needed for the tile, you'll get a better mosaic if the program can select an image that naturally meets the value and composition needed for a given tile. Purists will only use a tile once and not rotate images or change their exposures to force them to fit. The more pictures you take, the better the mosaic program will be able to fit the right valued picture into the composition. As a rule of thumb, I'd say aim for a bank at least twice the size of your intended tile count, and the more, the better!

Fair Terminology

In fairs and expositions, exhibits are entered according to *division* (such as "cattle," "antiques," or "cultural arts"), *class* (such as "Brown Swiss," "carnival glass" or "ceramics" and *lot* (such as "heifer calf, spring," "goblet," or "glazed item"). Many people will say *"class"* when they're actually talking about *"lot."*

You're probably wondering what I carry and how I carry it. As I said, in 2012, I carried a D60 SLR and a Z70 pocket digital (I say "pocket" digital rather than "point and shoot" because the important feature is the physical size and not how it shoots). Before I got my D60, the answer was usually my Nikon FG (later my Nikon N2020, also known as an F401), two lenses, and—depending on the specific shooting I planned—neutral density filters, star-cross filters, diffraction grating filters, a flash unit, a 35mm Horizont panoramic camera, and/or a tripod.

My first camera bag was an Ambico adjustable three-compartment with an outside pocket and interior cover pouch. It's still my preferred fair-going bag. I put the SLR in the center compartment lens down (it shares the space with my billfold). In what I think of as the "back" compartment (I carry it on my left side, because there's only a one-way zipper and it closes to the right, so that's the "front"), I put the other lens and either the Horizont if I want to take panoramas, the teleconverter if I want extra length (usually when I'm in the grandstand) or the flash if I want it for night pictures. The front compartment holds a refillable "souvenir" cup, which I usually fill with something before I head to the fair. Filters (most often polarizing, neutral densities, and diffusions) hang out in the cover pocket (and film, when I carried it), and the outer pouch sometimes has a pen and notebook, and usually fills up with trinkets from the 'dozer games. The Z70 goes in whatever nook or cranny it fits in. My tripod has a (video) camera grip on it, which I didn't take off because I discovered it makes a great hook; I hook it over the shoulder strap and let it settle down against the back of the bag, where it stays vertical and the length of the grip ensures it won't wriggle its way off the bag.

Situation 1: Inanimate Exhibits (Still life)

People can get into heated debates about what does and does not constitute a "still life." I've found one of the safest ways to think of them is as "portraits of inanimate objects." Like portraits, they can be carefully set up in a studio, or found casually out in the world.

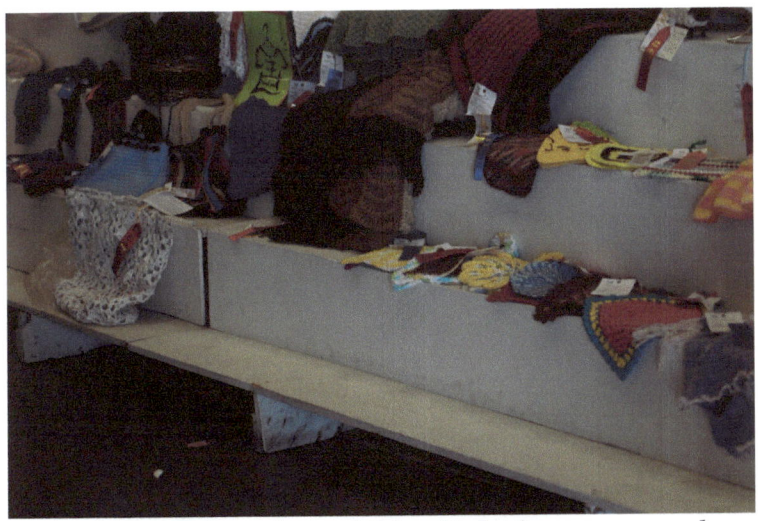

Judged knit and crochet exhibits. Light from an open door illuminates the closer potholders and dishcloths, but not the tote bags farther away. (D60: ISO-800, 1/160 sec, probably f/5.6, probably 50mm)

The various inanimate exhibits offer many convenient still lifes that don't even require setting up—the judge's assistants have done that for you in placing and arranging the displays.

If the exhibit buildings have skylights, exhibit areas can seem brighter to the eye than they are to the camera. Large entryways also create brighter areas, especially when they face the direction of the sun.

So there's a matter of timing when shooting in

buildings: Shoot exhibits near the doors when the sun is shining into them; shoot in early afternoon if the skylights help in lighting the exhibits you're interested in; and shoot toward evening if the skylights are putting your intended composition into shadow.

A flash can help in many of these situations, but be careful not to overuse it. In many cases, you're close enough that you only need a fraction of the flash's strength to brighten the area, and lower-end cameras will carelessly bleach the image at full strength.

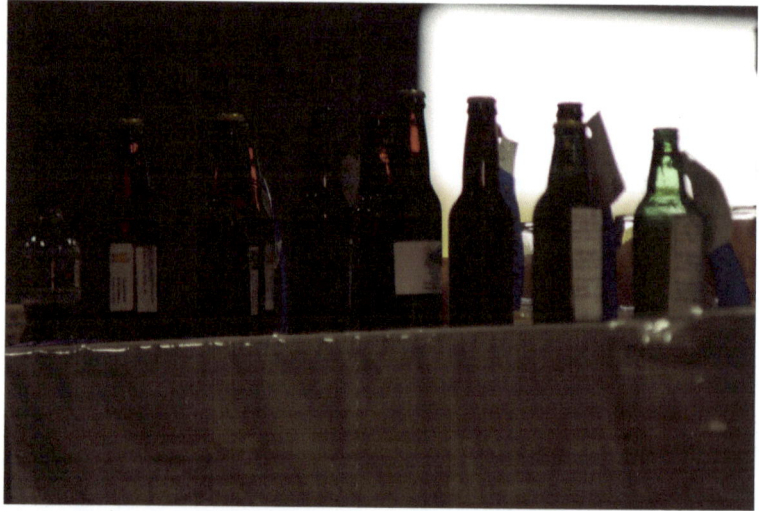

A great exercise in exposure control: A bright, sunlit doorway back-lighting half the scene, shadowed walls behind the other half, and (in this building, anyway) very high fluorescent bulbs that make for dim lighting as far as your camera's concerned. And though it may seem like a good place for a flash, it's actually on the far side for most flashes to reach. (D60:ISO-800, 1/50 sec, probably f/4, probably 210mm +2x converter)

Of course, sometimes you take the shots when you can get them. Sometimes the only time exhibits are out and easily seen is when they're being judged. In some departments, multiple lots migrate to and from the judge's table together and it's hard to follow what's going on unless you're familiar with the department. In other classes or departments, the judging itself becomes a show, with the judge miked and explaining his decisions as he goes along for exhibitors and casual spectators alike.

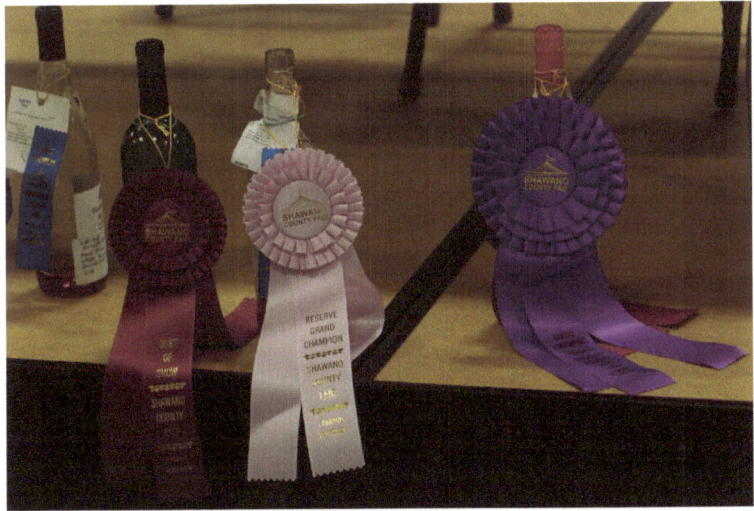

A scene you will only catch at judging time. Before this, there were no ribbons, in an hour or two they'll be crammed one behind another inside a refrigerated display case with condensation-filled glass spoiling your shot. (D60:ISO-800, 1/50 sec, probably f/5.6, probably 70 mm)

Situation 2: Animals

Animals in the barns have all the weird and wonderful lighting challenges of inanimate exhibits, plus they move, and you generally don't have the help of flash. *Never use flash around live exhibits unless their owner assures you they won't mind.*

Dog judging. The door on the far wall is the same door that's behind the wine bottles in the previous situation. Since it's closed, only the fluorescents illuminate the scene. (D60:ISO-800, 1/50 sec. probably f/5.6, probably 28 mm)

With large animals, it's often easier to wait until their designated judging time, where you can often get them in sunlight and not bunched up with other exhibits. Designated exercise (horses) or milking (cattle and dairy goats) times are also good times to catch them outside.

With small animals, judging time can be one of those spectator-unfriendly situations where you can't really get a good angle, so you're left with shooting them in their cages.

This is one of those situations where the pocket camera has an advantage over the SLR. The physical diameter of the lens is smaller than most cage wiring, so you can simply hold the camera at a point that puts the lens between the wires. While it's possible to shoot between the wires with an SLR lens, you're often limited to shooting straight through, and what may seem like a clean shot in the viewfinder may turn out to have wires in the frame or out-of-focus areas caused by unseen-but-close-enough-to-cause-lensing wires just out of frame.

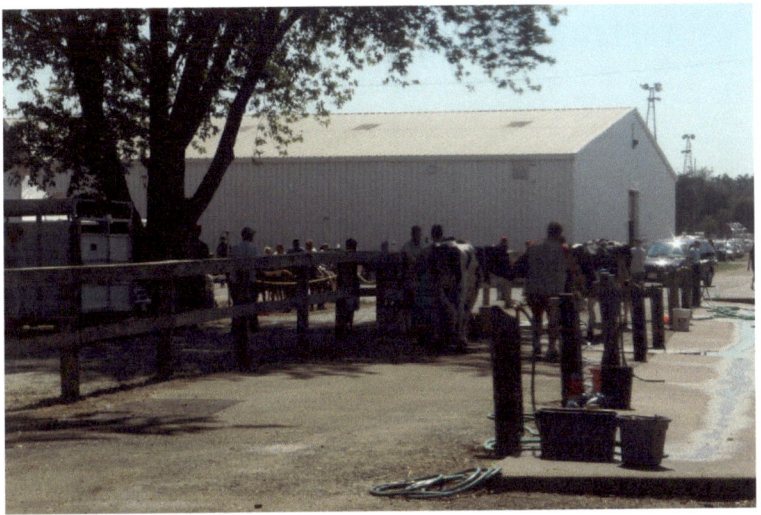

It's easier to get a good look at cattle when they're outside getting groomed, watered, or waiting for their turn in the show ring or milking parlor. (D60:IS0-800, 1/100 sec, probably f/11, probably 35 mm)

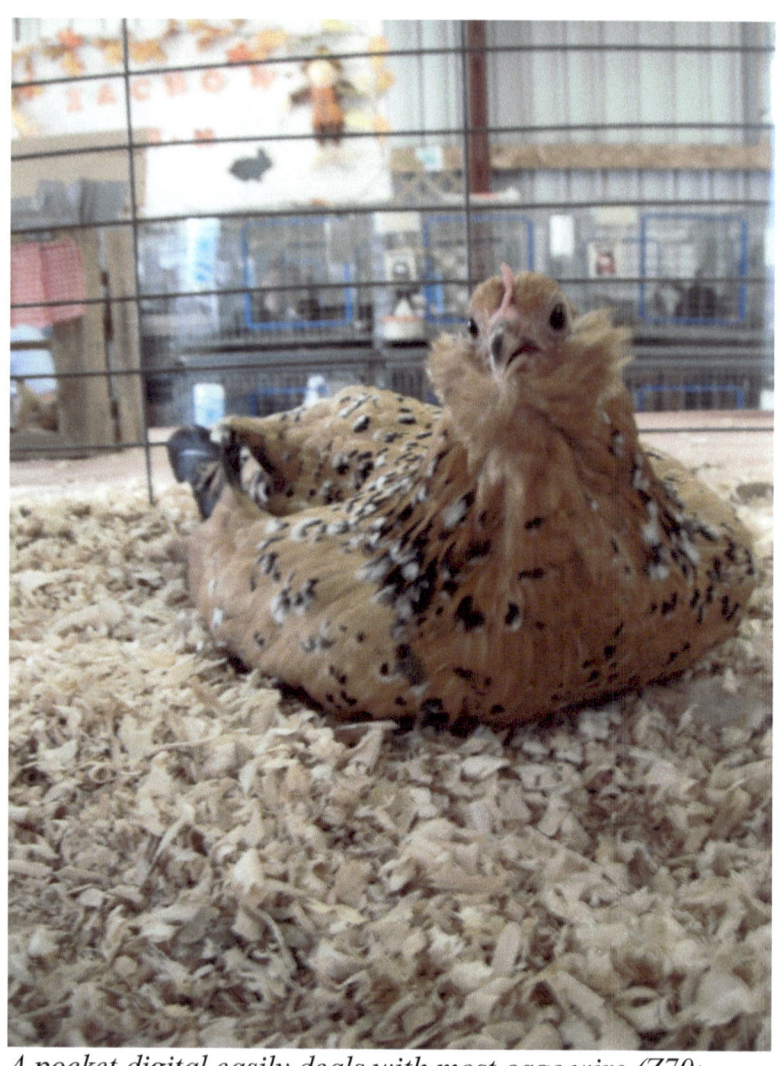

A pocket digital easily deals with most cage wire (Z70: ISO-100, 1/5 sec, f/4)

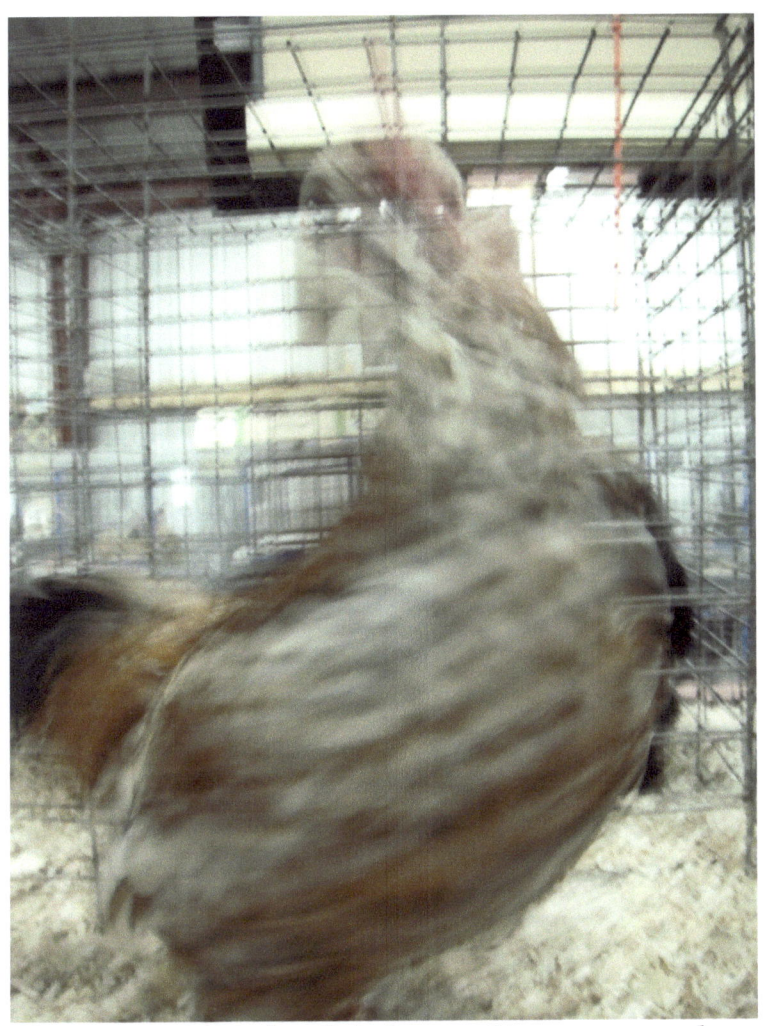

The unique way pocket digitals record images can make for some interesting abstracts. In this case, the camera recorded the body, the bird moved its head, and then the camera recorded the head, making the bird look like the subject of a magician's "saw-it-in-half" trick. (Z70:ISO-400, 1 sec, f/4)

Situation 3: In the Grandstand

Depending on what event you're watching, the grandstand can be a great place to work on long-distance action, panning shots, and dealing with obstructions. Depending on where the grandstand is relative to the rest of the fairgrounds, it can also be a great vantage point for above-the-crowd midway shots.

Selecting your vantage point requires some thought. If you're in the grandstand to watch stock car racing or other motor sports, a low position in the stands will leave you frustrated by the inevitable safety fencing.

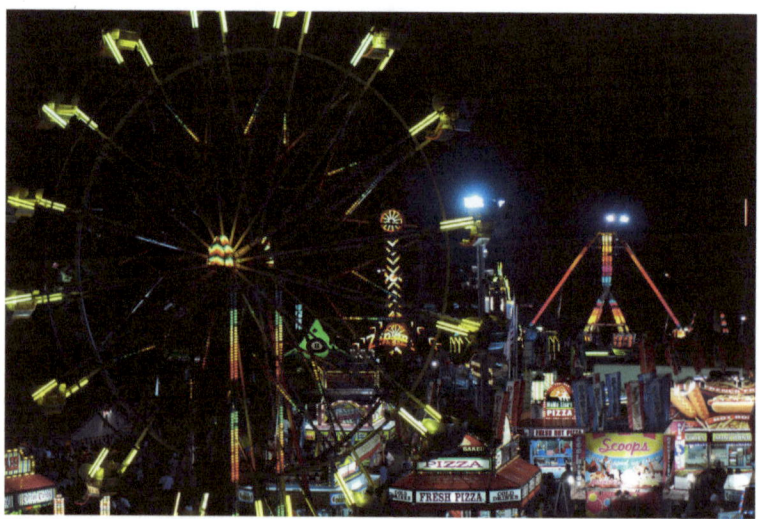

The midway as seen looking north from the grandstand. (D60: ISO-800, 1/60 sec, probably f/5.6, probably 50 mm)

I've found a position high enough to see most of the track over the safety fencing, on one end of the grandstand so you have a relatively unobstructed view of at least one corner, and hopefully without someone sitting directly in front of you offers the most shooting options.

At the Shawano Speedway, the half mile of red clay lies north-south in the classic shape that horsemen count as having two turns and motor-sportsmen count as having four. The grandstand sits toward the north end of the front stretch, facing east and backing against the southern end of the midway. By taking a position high in the northernmost section, I can get a fair view of Turn 1, a decent view of Turn 2 exiting to the backstretch, and a pretty good view of Turns 3 and 4 up until just before the grandstand. And if the action gets boring on the track, I can turn around and get some good views of the midway.

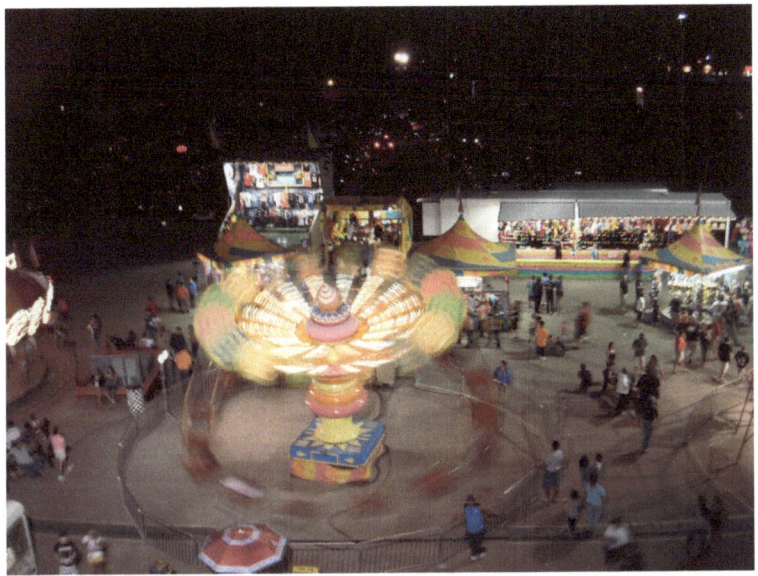

Kiddy land from the grandstand. An SLR wouldn't be able to get the necessary angle without the chain-link fencing fouling the shot, but a compact camera can fit completely through the links for an unobstructed shot. Unfortunately, the Z70 unoverrridably overexposes the shot in situations like this. (Z70: ISO-100, 1/4 sec, f/4)

If the event is midday, you can shoot anywhere you feel like and it won't make much difference. If the sun is going down, though, you'll want to adjust your shooting schedule to be taking your longest-distance images first, and switch to shorter lenses as the light fades. And don't bother with a flash, there isn't a hand-held flash built that can illuminate even the front stretch from the stands, much less the backstretch. A flash in the stands is only useful for taking bleached-out pictures of the backs of people's heads.

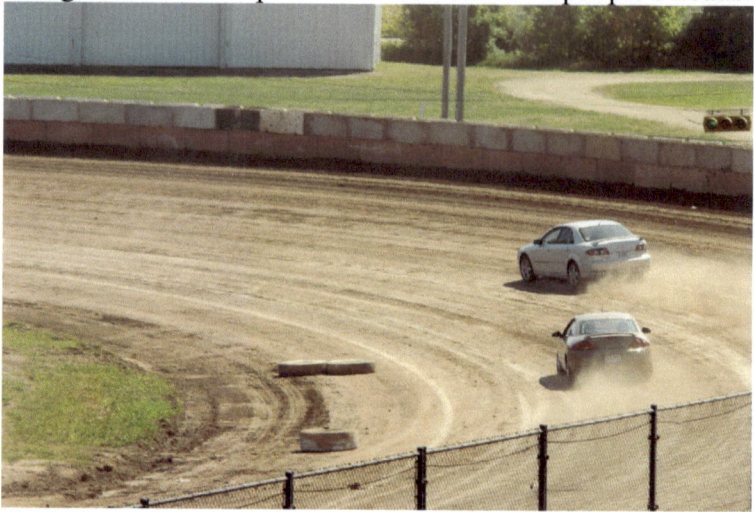

Spectator eliminators (street cars) going into Turn 1.The fencing can easily be cropped away. (D60: ISO-800, 1/200 sec, probably f/8, probably 210 mm w/ 2x converter)

So, since longer lenses need more light, I shoot the most distant scenes first. If you're lucky, you can catch some passing action between turns one and two or coming out of turn two.

As the setting sun puts the front stretch and turn one into the shadow of the grandstand and fencing, I shift my attention to the backstretch and Turn 3. These are closer and I can use the shorter end of my 70-210 mm lens, giving me one more f-stop.

By the time the sun actually sets, it's dark enough that to keep a practical shutter speed, I have to take the teleconverter off and shoot with the 70-210 mm by itself.

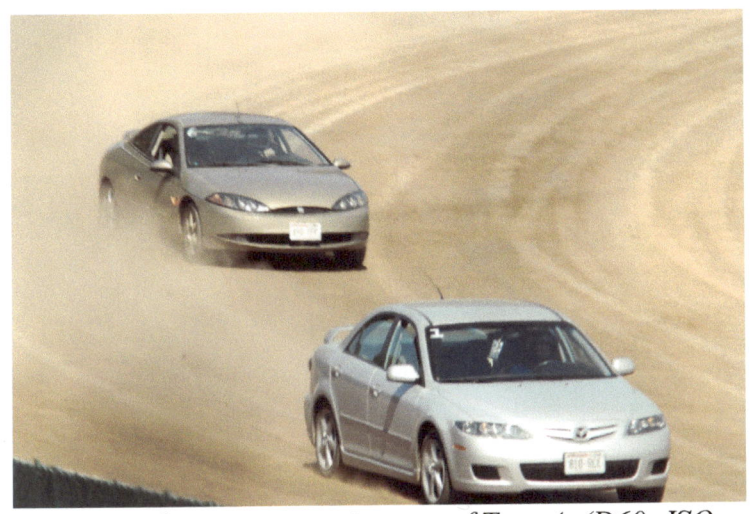

Spectator eliminators coming out of Turn 4. (D60: ISO-800, 1/200 sec, probably f/11, probably 210 mm w/2x converter)

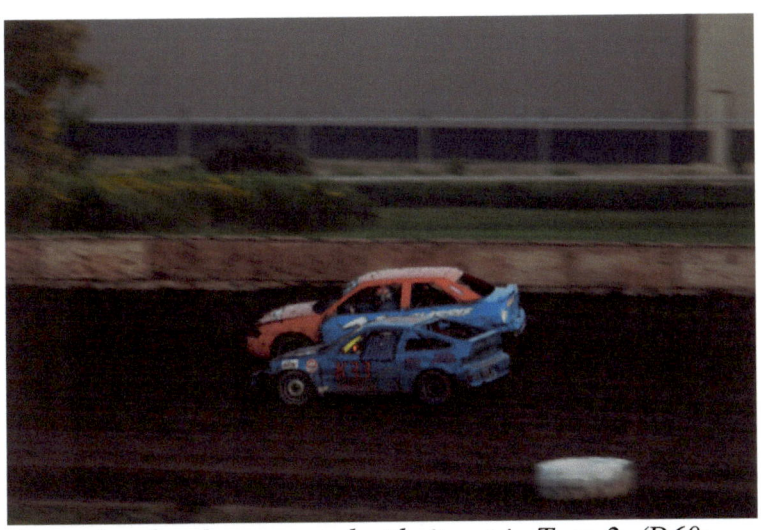

A couple of enduro racers battle it out in Turn 2. (D60: ISO-800, 1/80 sec, probably f/4, 210 mm w/2x converter)

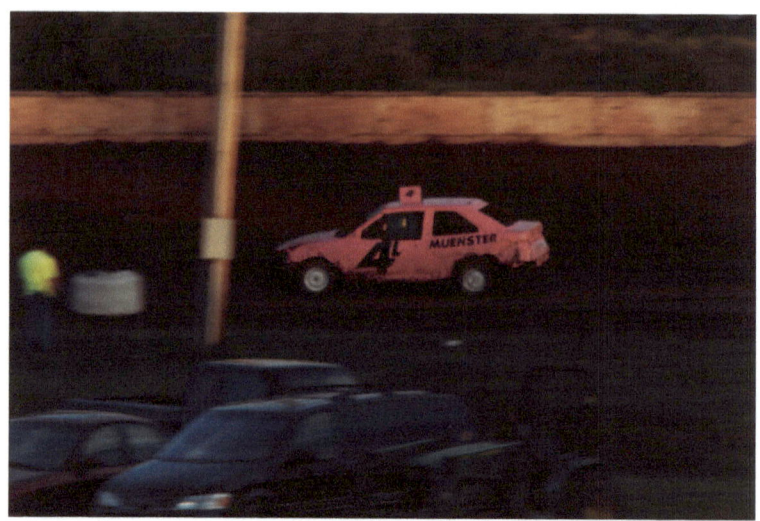

An enduro racer coming out of Turn 2. The long shadows indicate that Turn 1 is already too shadowed for good shots, and soon it will be time to take the converter off. Panning with the action can buy some time. (D60: ISO-800, 1/80 sec, probably f/5.6, probably 200mm w/2x converter)

I'll use the last rays of daylight to catch the action in Turn 4 and the top of the front stretch.

Eventually the light will get so low that "point and

How slow is too slow?

Most experts will advise you not shoot hand-held at a speed lower than the reciprocal of the focal length, e.g. 1/60 sec (the closest shutter setting to 1/50 sec in most cameras) if you're shooting a 50mm lens. I'll often shoot as slow as 1/30, even with a long lens, accepting that some shots might be lost to blur or camera shake. I take a page from my middle-school BB-gun course in gym class: Exhale, stop breathing, shoot, inhale. You're more likely to move if you try to hold your lungs full of air.

---

click" just doesn't give the lens enough light, even if the track seems to have decent lighting. It's a great opportunity to work on panning shots.

Panning is something I never tried with my film cameras, but most digitals (SLR's, at least) are smart enough to figure out what you're doing and help you out.

Enduros battling between Turns 1 and 2. Definitely time to take the converter off. Although this can be salvaged by post-processing, it's really too dark to be shooting at this distance anymore. (D60: ISO-800, 1/60 sec, probably f/5.6, 210 mm w/2x converter)

Panning action shots are also a great way to deal with that annoying safety fencing: While you can't do anything about the horizontal supports, the chain link simply disappears and the only thing you have to worry about is timing your shot to avoid the vertical posts.

I usually shoot panning action at 1/30 sec with my 28-70 mm lens. Pick your subject, start panning to keep it in frame, push the shutter when it's where you want, and follow it through until you can't. And hope you didn't open the shutter while your subject was behind one of the posts.

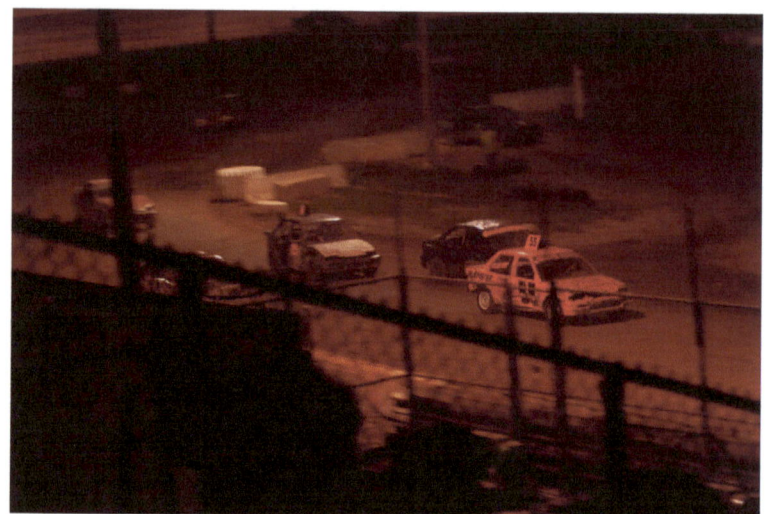

Enduros coming out of Turn 4. Closer subjects make it easier for exposure, but harder for composition. Track safety fencing, grandstand railing/fencing, and a nearby building all work to limit the angles that allow a clear shot. (D60: ISO-800, 1/60, probably f/4, probably 70 mm)

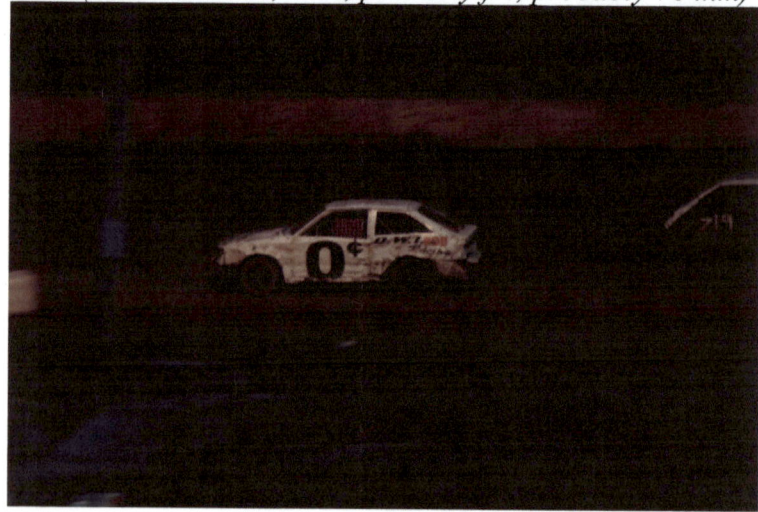

Lighter colored subjects can also buy a shutter step or two. (D60: ISO-800, 1/60 sec, probably f/4, probably 210 mm w/ 2x converter)

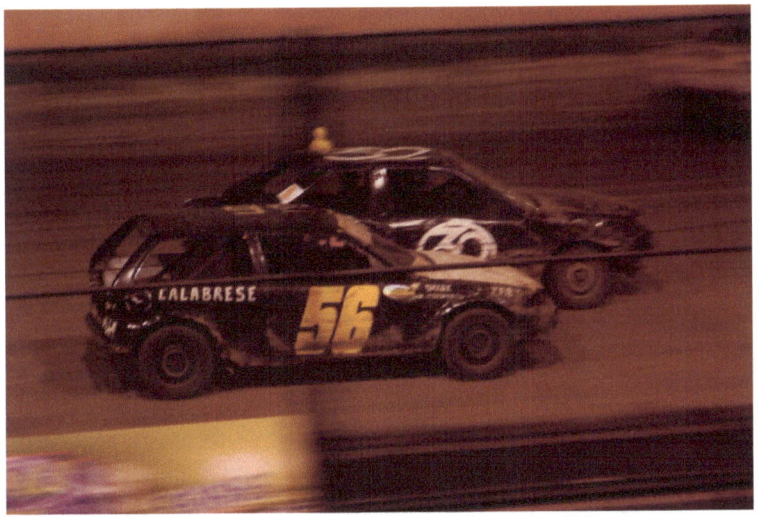

This one didn't quite miss the post, though if the cars were going faster, we might not even see it. The chain link has simply disappeared. (D60: ISO-800, 1/30 sec, probably f/3.5, probably 70mm)

So what mode do I use?

The list of program modes for most cameras doesn't include "night action (distant)." So what setting do you use? The basic "night" mode gives your camera free rein to use its flash, which is useless in this kind of situation. "Sport" tells it to pick a shutter speed fast enough to freeze the action, which is another excuse for your camera to go to its flash. The best choice is likely going to be "landscape," which warns the camera that the subject is too far away for the flash.

(I actually ran into this in Milwaukee: I had borrowed my aunt's point-and-shoot 35mm and tried to shoot fireworks from my dorm room. It didn't have a "fireworks" mode, and selecting "night" rewarded me with a huge glare off the dorm window)

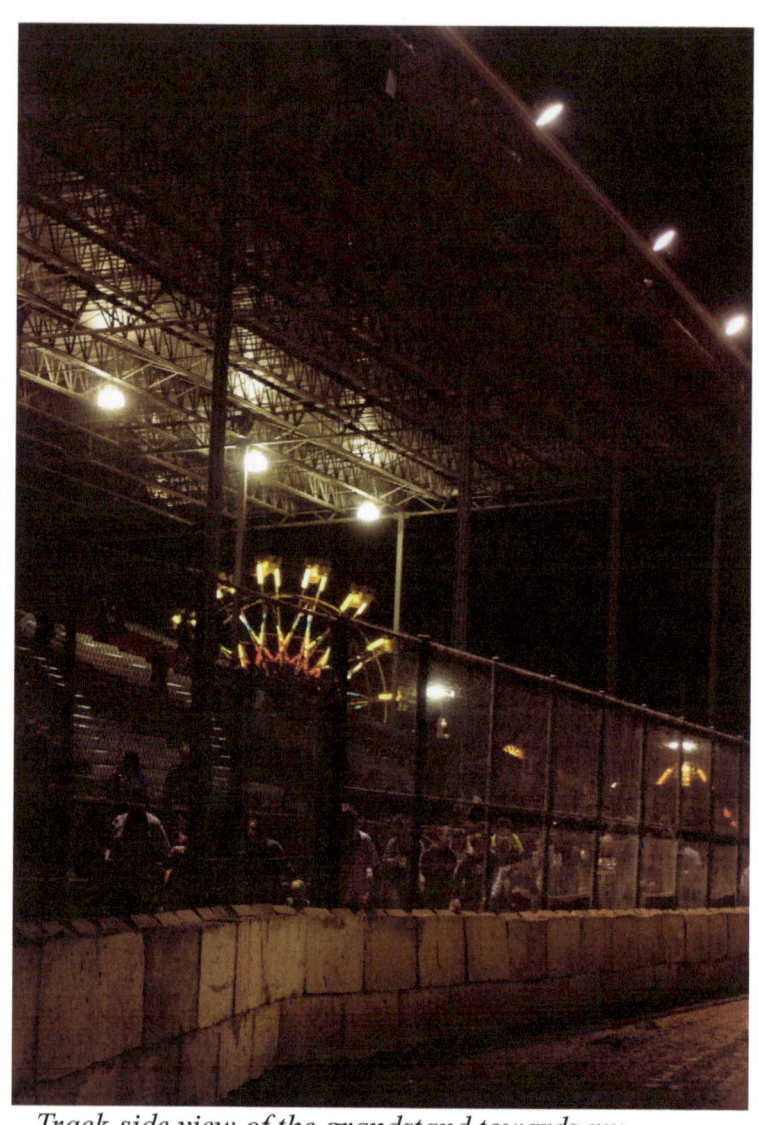

*Track-side view of the grandstand towards my
favorite shooting spot. (D60: probably ISO-800,
1/100 sec, probably f/5.6, probably 120 mm)*

Situation #4: The Midway

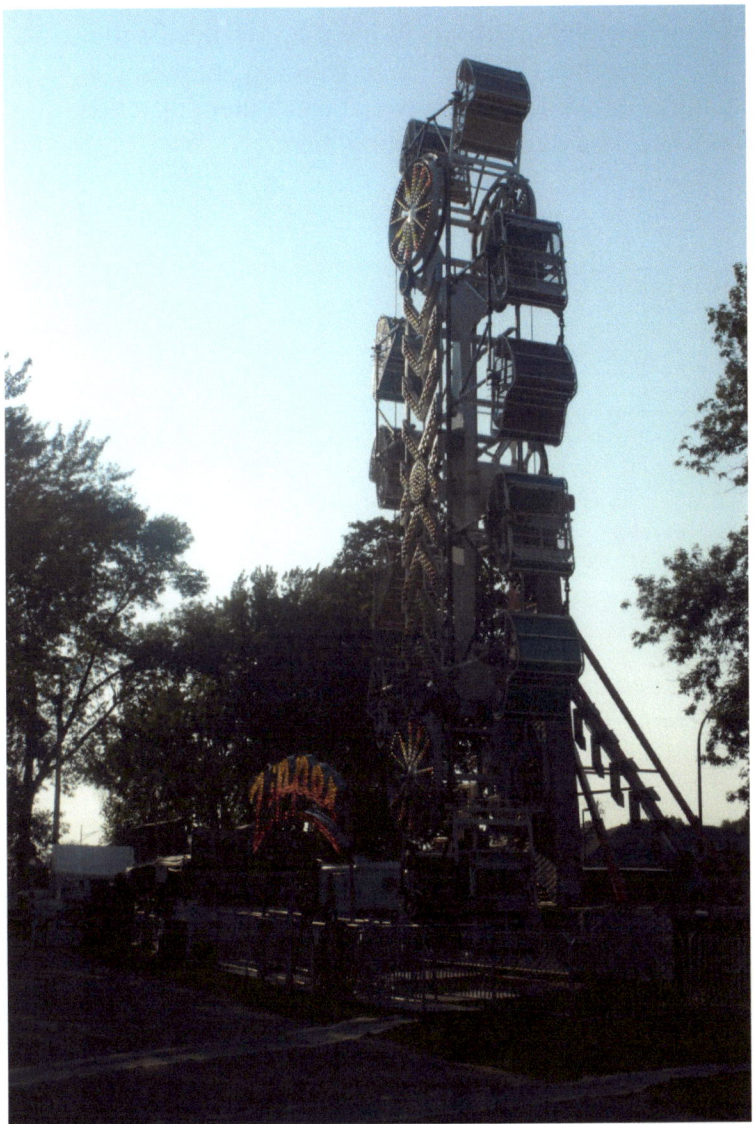

With no crowds, one can take portraits of the rides. (D60: ISO-800, 1/250 sec, probably f/11, probably 50 mm)

Many people's favorite part of the fair (mine included) is the midway. When the crowds are low, one can always take stately portraits of the rides, or details to use for later reference (if you're in to painting or making miniatures or such), but you won't catch them in action unless somebody's actually riding them.

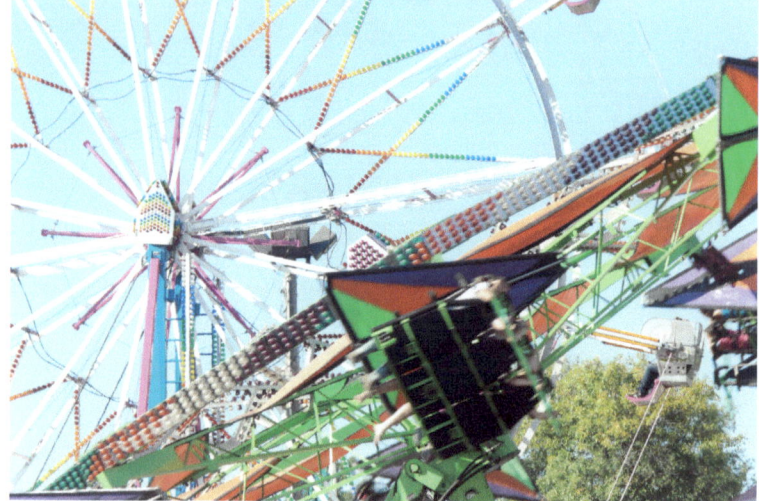

You can't catch a ride in action unless someone's riding it. (Well, sometimes you can bribe the operator to give it a turn or two fro your camera). Cliff Hanger in action. (D60: ISO-800, 1/160 sec, probably f/11, probably 210 mm)

Rides such as the Ferris Wheel or fun house don't look much different whether they're moving or not (at least in the daytime). But most rides are a lot more interesting when they're moving. Sometimes the best parts of rides don't even show unless they're moving. That means you need people around to ride the rides.

Then there's the matter of shutter speeds. Like the motor sports discussed in the grandstand section, you can choose a shutter speed to stop the action, and you can

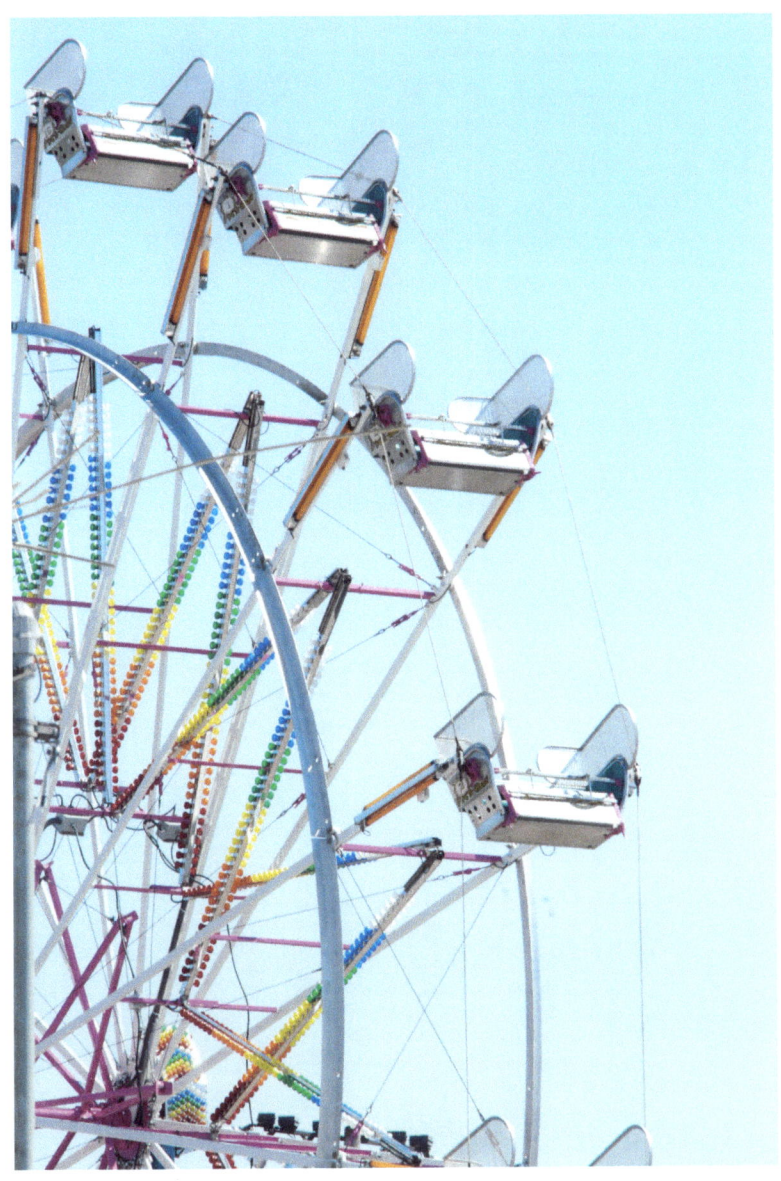

The Pleasure (i.e. "Ferris") Wheel is often the tallest ride on the midway (or close to it), and every carnival company has one. Yet shooting it never gets old. (D60: ISO-800, 1/160 sec, probably f/11, probably 120 mm)

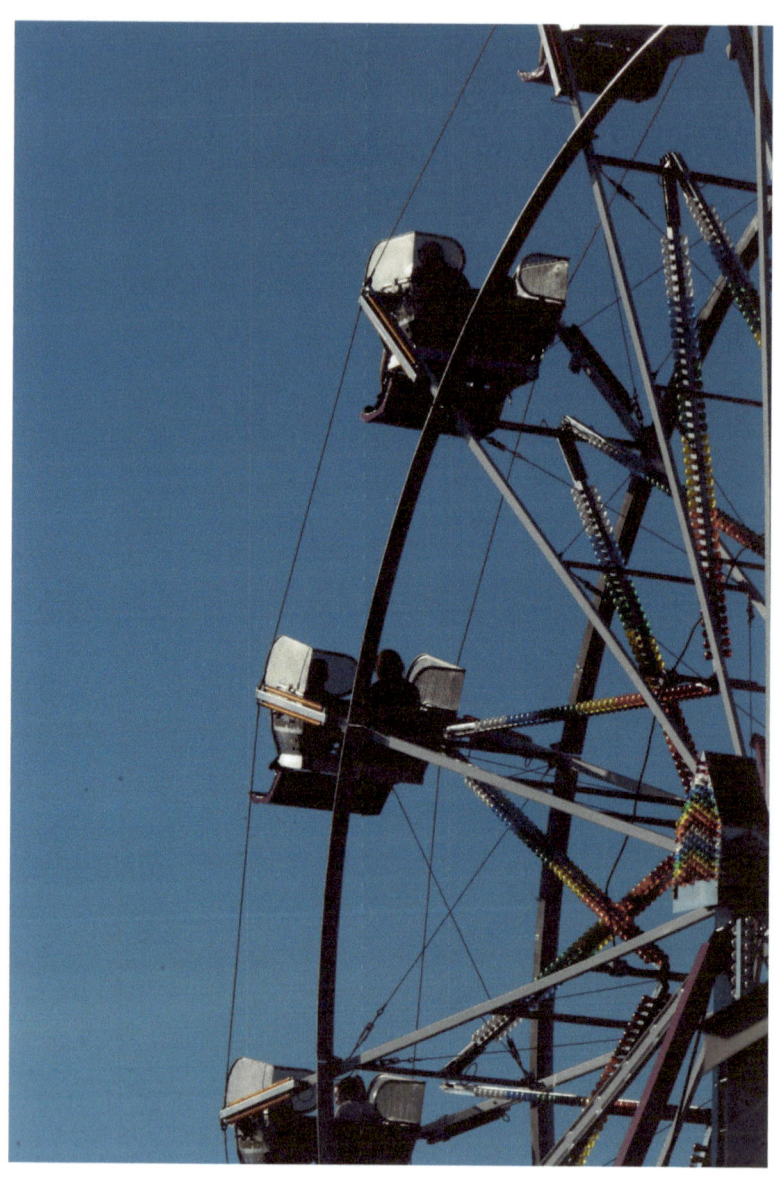

Ferris wheels offer plenty to shoot when they're standing still, but riders make a more interesting picture than empty cars. (D60:ISO-800, 1/400, probably f/11, probably 150 mm)

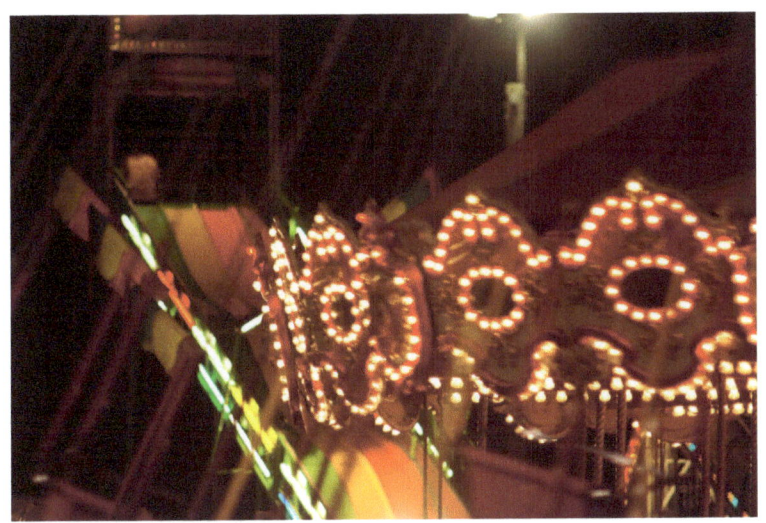

This image of the carrousel was shot through the chains of the moving Lollipop Swings in order to break up the sharpness and create a more dreamy, impressionistic view. The carrousel uses incandescent bulbs, the Super Slide behind it has colored fluorescents. (D60:ISO-800, 1/60 sec, probably f/11, probably 210 mm)
choose to *not* stop the action. You can deliberately allow the subject to blur, or pan with the subject and allow everything else to blur.

But the greatest use of shutter speed is night, when the midway presents situations you're not likely to encounter anywhere else. Because at night the lights come on.

Lighting can vary greatly from ride to ride and even within a single ride. Early lighting was simple tungsten (incandescent). In the 1960s and '70s, fluorescent tubes tended to dominate lighting schemes. Then in the '80s, "jewel" lighting (a small bulb in a plastic, gem-like housing) became common, and since the turn of the millennium, LED's have come into vogue.

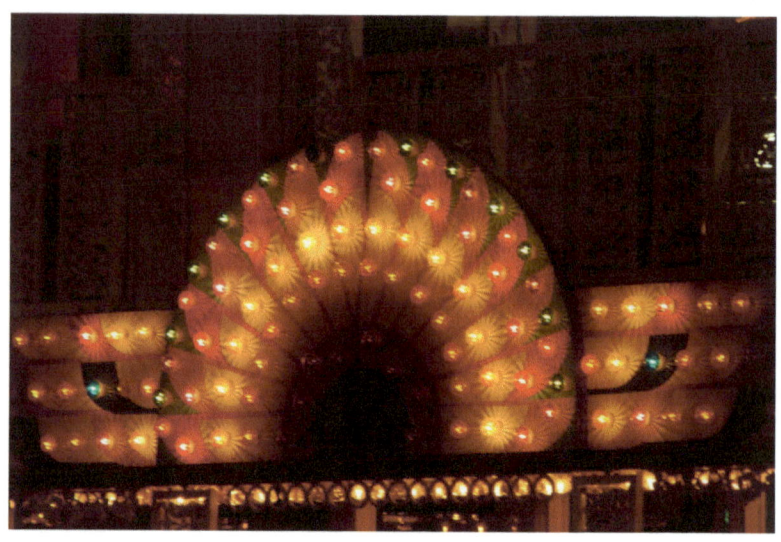

Detail of the Mardi Gras (a "fun house") showing "jewel" lighting. (D60: ISO-800, 1/50 sec, probably f/5.6, probably 70 mm)

Ride Lights Aren't
Just for Decoration.

Many times the last day of a fair or festival doesn't end until well after sunset, and carnival companies must be rolling before dawn to make their next event (And they'd rather be rolling when there's less traffic). After the fairgrounds shut their lights off, often the only light to pack up by comes from the rides themselves.

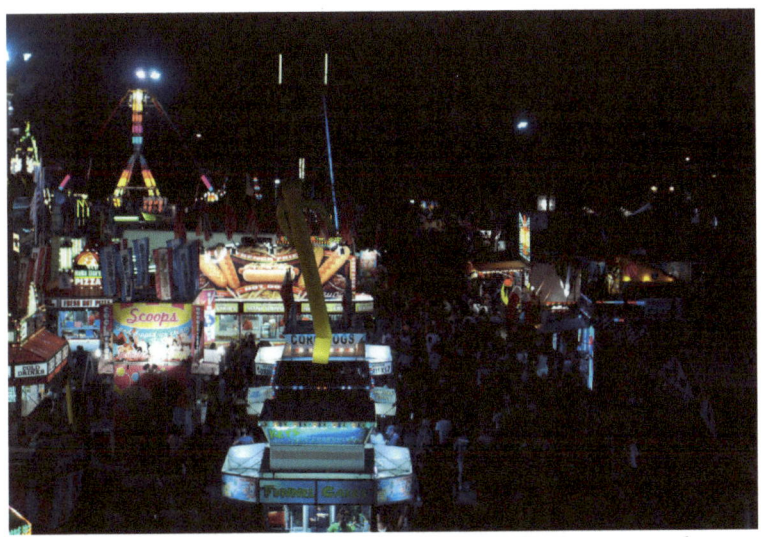

View of the midway from the grandstand. The two rides visible in back are Freak Out (jewel-lamped) and the uprights of Pharaoh's Fury (fluorescent tubes). Pharaoh's Fury was re-lamped the next year in LED's. (D60: ISO-800, 1/60 sec, probably f/8, probably 210 mm)

Pharaoh's Fury (D60: ISO-800, 1/200 sec, probably f/11, probably 210 mm w/2x converter)

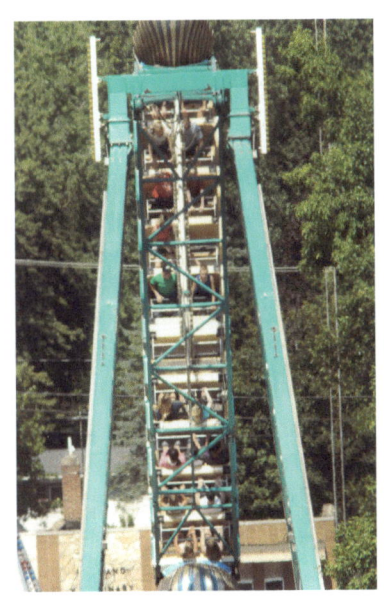

This can make the right white balance . . . interesting. The grounds lighting is likely sodium vapor or mercury vapor (those are types of fluorescent, but not ones every camera recognizes). For overall scenes, it tends to come down to a matter of taste: Nearly any lighting scene can seem "right" if you only have the picture to look at and can't compare it to the real scene or a similar photo with different white balance settings. I usually prefer warmth of daylight balance. I like the warmer feel and find that the skies tend to be blacker than with other white balances, which tend to allow more of a haze from lamps to creep into the sky. (And I'm often too lazy to switch from daylight after the sun goes down, but I will occasionally play with white balance in overall scenes.)

You may or may not have to be more careful about white balance when you're focusing on a particular ride. Tungsten actually hasn't been that common on the midway

---

The Link Between
Ferris Wheels and Midways

When Chicago planned the 1893 Columbian Exposition, they wanted something to top France's Eiffel Tower from the Paris Exposition. After repeatedly rejecting the idea of a giant pleasure wheel from and engineer named George Ferris, they finally agreed to let him build it. There was controversy between genteel groups that wanted the Fair to be a thing of culture and beauty and the investors that knew it was the common man's patronage that would put the Fair in the black. The solution was to create the Midway Plaisance to put the more vulgar attractions in, including the giant pleasure wheel. Midways and Ferris wheels have been a perennial part of fairs ever since.

---

for decades, mostly showing up on the carrousel. Jewel lamps seen relatively unaffected by white balance settings, especially if there aren't many white-colored ones. The tricky situation comes with fluorescents, which amusement rides use in colors no camera is prepared to record.

The trickiest ride to shoot lighting-wise I've found is the Tilt-A-Whirl. Not only is it illuminated exclusively by fluorescents, but it uses two different temperature "white" tubes, which look like they're the same color when shot in most white-balance settings. I shot every white-balance setting on my D60 trying to get the difference to show, finally deciding "mercury vapor" worked the best.

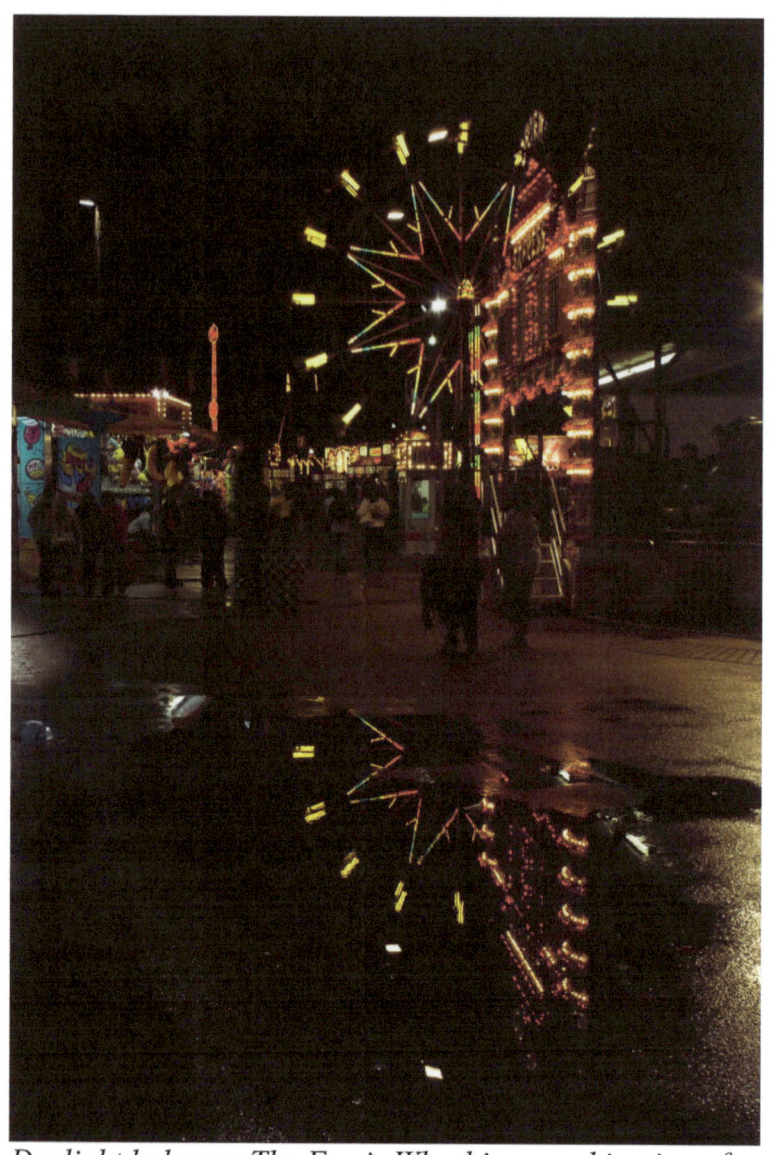

Daylight balance: The Ferris Wheel is a combination of jewels (center) and fluorescents (outside). Orient Express (foreground) has jewel-lamped façade. (D60: ISO-800, 1/30 sec, probably f/11, probably 70 mm)

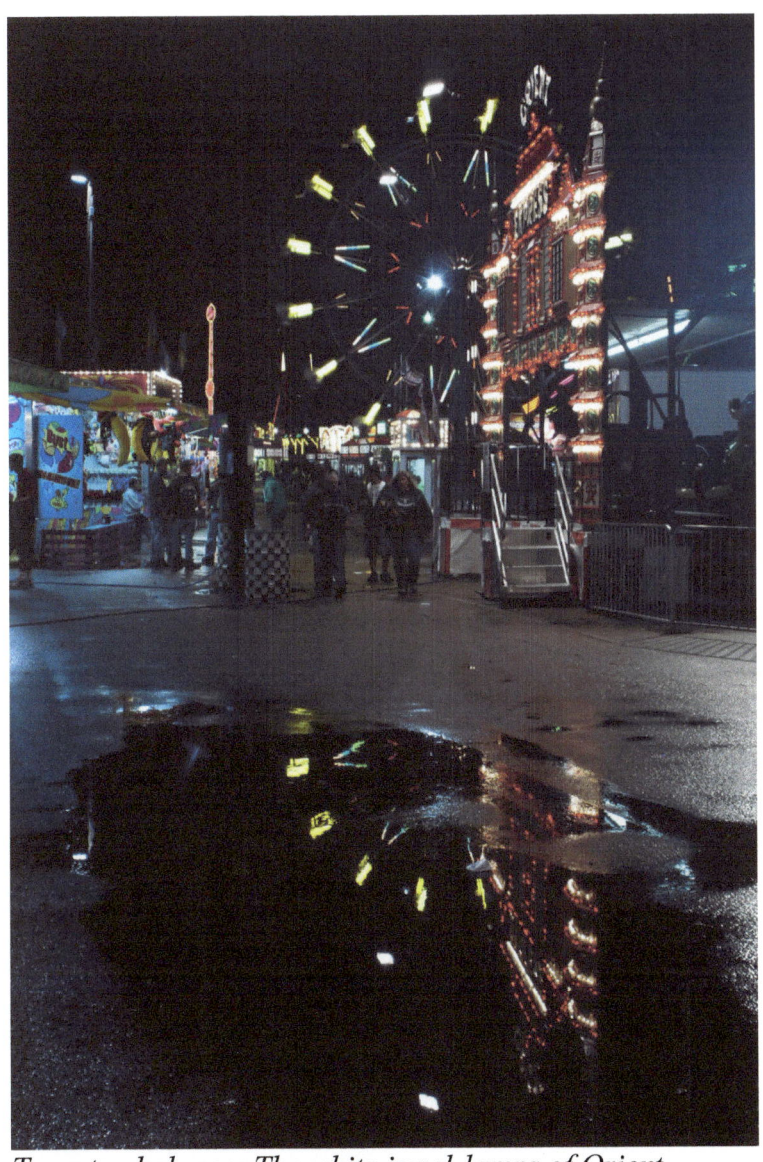

Tungsten balance: The white jewel-lamps of Orient Express are notably cooler, and there is a haze around the fluorescents illuminating the boarding area. (D60: same settings)

My favorite ways to shoot anything at the fair happen to be the only techniques that absolutely require a tripod. Even a lightweight tripod will get heavy enough if you're carrying it all over the midway, so don't bother with one that's heavy to begin with. You can always hold it down if you need to.

(Confession: Since my 2012 shots of this type were all on the lost card, I've resorted to some of my 2011 pictures. And when the camera is set to "bulb," it records the time the shutter is open decimally, not fractionally.)

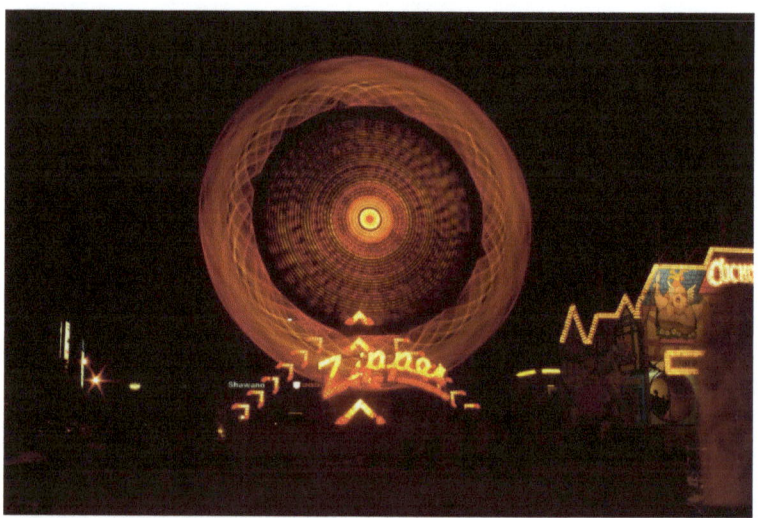

Some call Zipper a "Ferris Wheel freak," The circular light pattern could almost pass for a simple wheel, and a slower shutter speed might convince you it is. But the exposure didn't last an exact number of revolutions, so some parts of the circle were more heavily exposed than others. (D60: ISO-100, 8 sec, probably f/22, probably 35 mm)

Capturing a ride's "light tracks" is fun and easy, but not all rides are good candidates for the technique; you want rides that have lighting on the parts that move the most, which makes for great abstracts. You can have great fun turning wheels (Ferris or otherwise) and carrousels into disks of concentric color. Even more fun are rides that have more complex motions.

Timing is also something to consider. If there are no crowds, the rides aren't moving. If the crowds are too dense, you won't get a clear view of your chosen ride. Check the fair schedule. If you live in a cheapskate area, you might need a time when there are special ride prices to make sure the rides will be in motion (though this is less of an issue at night than it is in the daytime). If you don't, you might want to avoid those times, because the midway will likely be packed. If that's the case, pick a time when there are lots of other events going on.

When I first started shooting, there were only two special ride price times. Saturday nights were so packed, I did my tripod fun on other nights. As more ride discount sessions were added to the schedule, Saturday night crowds got a lot thinner, at least while the stock cars were racing, and it came to be a pretty good night for tripod shooting.

When I shot with film, I would try to have some ISO-100 on hand—slower if I could find it—and usually put some neutral density filters on the lens. I'd crank the aperture down as far as it went (f/22 or f/32, depending on the lens), and usually put the shutter to bulb, holding it open "about so long."

With digital, I set it to ISO-100, crank the aperture down, and set the shutter to anywhere between 1.5 and 8 seconds. I don't usually bother with filters. My D60 has so many shutter increments I shot with it quite a while before realizing it even *had* a bulb setting.

Another fun tripod technique doesn't even require the rides to move, what you're moving is the zoom ring on your lens. With this technique, you obviously need a zoom lens, preferably with an easy, smooth motion that maintains

43

a constant focus as you move the zoom through its range (not all zooms can be relied on to do this). I usually use my 28-70 mm Sigma because I can't get far enough away to keep the ride in frame at both ends of my 70-210 mm, and because the effect is stronger with a lens that can go from wide-angle to telephoto.

Set up your shot with the zoom lens on its wide end and smallest aperture. Hit the shutter, pause a beat, then zoom to the other end of its range and let go of the shutter. Depending on the length your shutter stays open, you'll end up with either radial rays coming away from the ride or a tunnel of light.

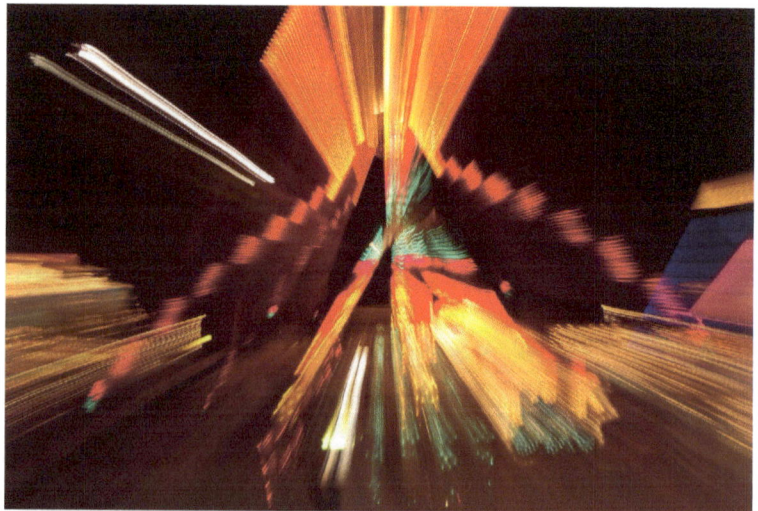

Zooming exposure of Freak Out at rest. There are plug-in filters that can do this. Sort of. (D60: ISO-100, 0.77 sec, probably f/22, 28-70 zoom)

There are plug-ins filters available for your digital darkroom that can do something like this to stationary objects, but can they do it with a moving ride?

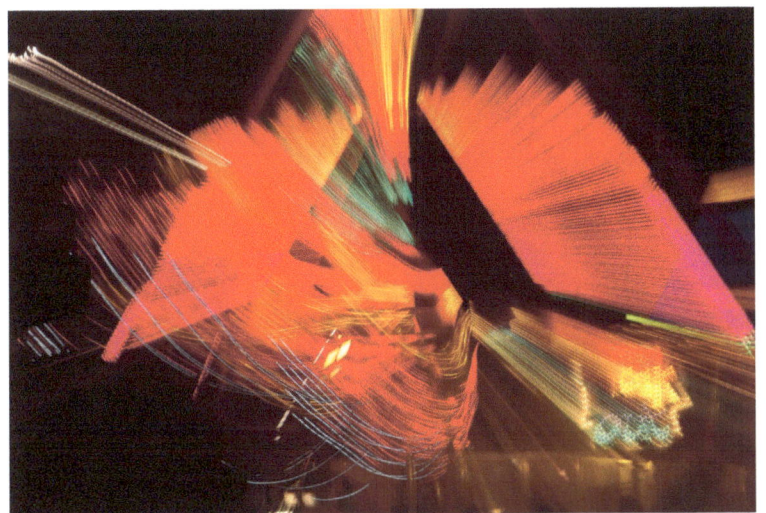

*In this case, Freak Out was swinging when I shot it.
(D60: ISO-100, 0.62 sec, probably f/22, 28-70 mm zoom)*

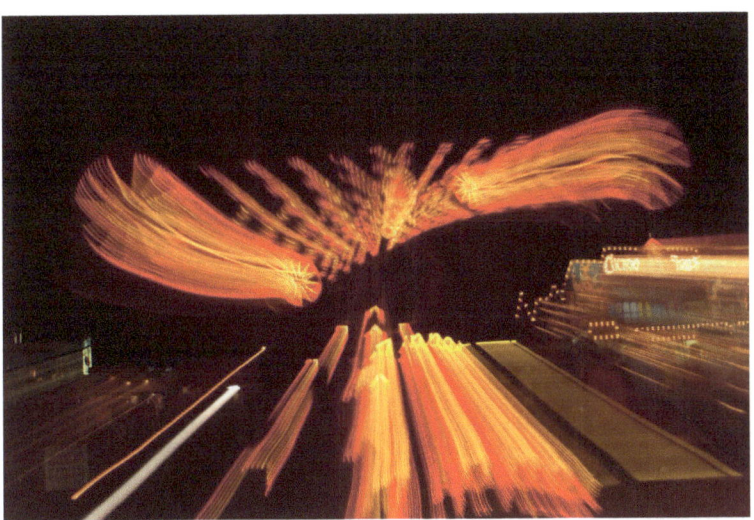

*Zipper, this time zooming while the ride was in motion.
(D60: ISO-100, 0.77 sec, probably f/22, 28-70 mm zoom)*

Flash Synchronization

The flash usually doesn't fire as long as the shutter stays open. So when during the exposure does it fire?

The cheap answer (and the one used by most cameras, pocket or SLR) is "front-synch," where the flash fires when the shutter opens. The more difficult answer, limited to higher-end SLR's, is "rear-synch," where the camera calculates the difference between the shutter time and the flash time, opens the shutter, waits that difference, and *then* fires the flash—so the flash will end as the shutter closes.

How does this affect your picture? Imagine a car driving by at night. The tail lights are bright enough to leave "light tracks" without the flash, but the car itself will only be bright enough to show when the flash is firing. If the flash fires at the beginning of the exposure, the light tracks caused by its taillights will overlap the car. If the flash fires at the end of the exposure, the light tracks will appear behind the car.

You can create a "poor man's" version of this by setting your camera to bulb, opening the shutter, and then—when your subject is where you want it—manually firing a hand-held or tripod mounted flash that is completely independent of the camera just before you release the shutter. You'll need a pretty strong flash to make it work.

One Last Picture

There is one last picture you have to consider when shooting for a mosaic, and that is the main image for the mosaic itself. Ideally this will be a fairly simple image, as the more complex it gets, the harder it will be to see it among the images making up the mosaic, but it also needs to have enough variation in it that the program won't be selecting exclusively from one type of image (e.g. a very white main image wouldn't be a good choice if you had mostly night scenes.)

What do you think of when you think of "fair"? Being in dairy country, a cow comes to my mind, but since I don't have a lot of animal pictures, it doesn't fit that well. I also considered a ribbon, but couldn't come up with a photo that made it clear that it was a ribbon without leaving it so simplistic that only a limited selection of my images would fit it (maybe that's a problem you'll solve).

The more I thought about the fair and the images used on fair posters, the more I decided on a carrousel horse.

In 2011, I went through my image bank after the fair and picked out a nice head shot of a carrousel horse. In 2012, I deliberately composed a head shot with the horse facing the other way, so I could have a "book match" pair.

Got a few hundred pictures?
OK, Now let's make a mosaic.

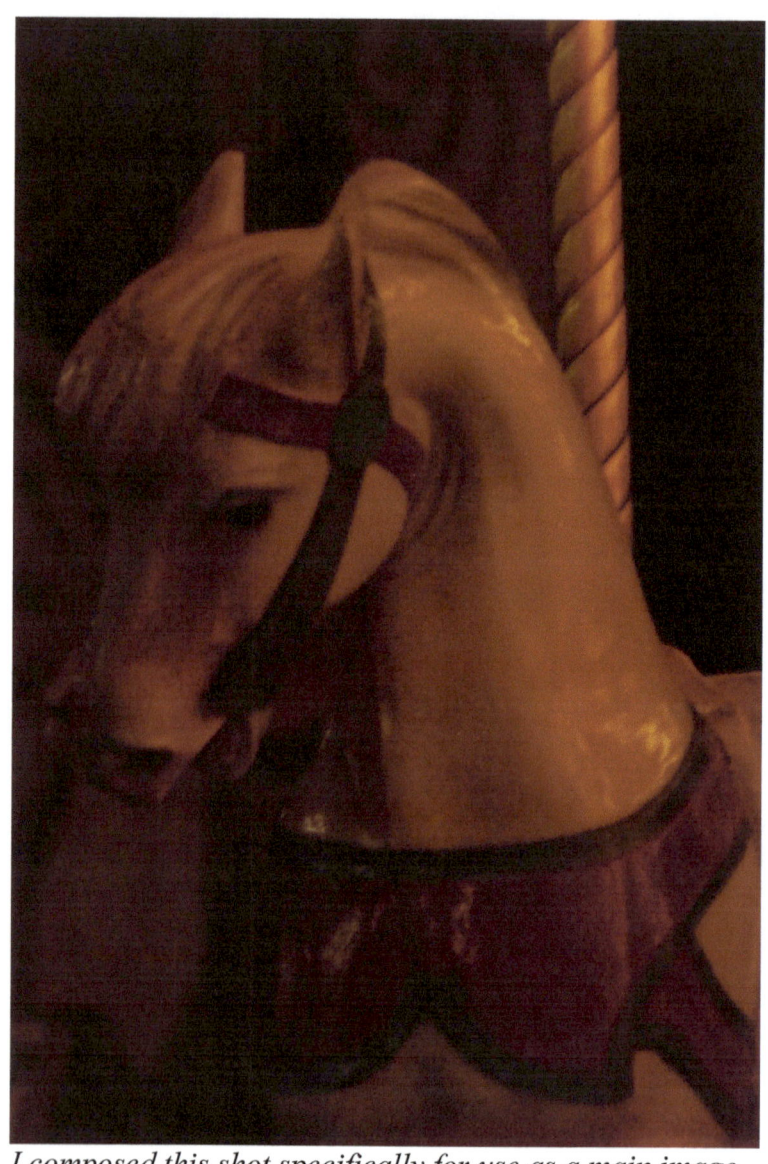

*I composed this shot specifically for use as a main image.
(D60: ISO-800, 1/60 sec, probably f/5.6 probably 70 mm)*

Part II: Making the Mosaic

This tutorial uses the free version of AndreaMosaic. If you've found a different mosaic-creating program, some terms and fields may be different, but you shouldn't have too much trouble translating the ideas.

Now that your photo library is assembled, AndreaMosaic needs to analyze the images and create a list of available tiles. For the 772 images in this tutorial, that took about an hour on a single-core laptop.

Now you have to decide what kind of mosaic you want to create. Since I originally made this for a 4" x 6" photo album, I chose that for my mosaic size. For photo-quality printing 300 dots per inch is often considered the minimum. For viewing electronically, 72 dpi is enough. I picked a tile size of 1/2" because I though anything bigger would make it too hard to see the main image, and anything smaller would make it hard to see what the individual tiles were.

Next, you have to decide whether to allow AndreaMosaic to re-use tiles in more than one place, and if so, how often. Purists take a certain pride in using tiles only once in a mosaic, but if your library is on the small side, you may need to in order to fill the entire mosaic and/or avoid having the program force terribly inappropriate images into a position simply because it was the only tile available. I had enough images that I didn't think I had to allow the program to re-use them.

Tile pattern depends mostly on your ratio of landscape (horizontal) orientation images to portrait (vertical) orientation. (Or it may not be a factor if you allow the program to rotate the tiles.) I chose "Mixed2 (3.3L 1P)" because I had four to six times as many landscapes as I had portraits.

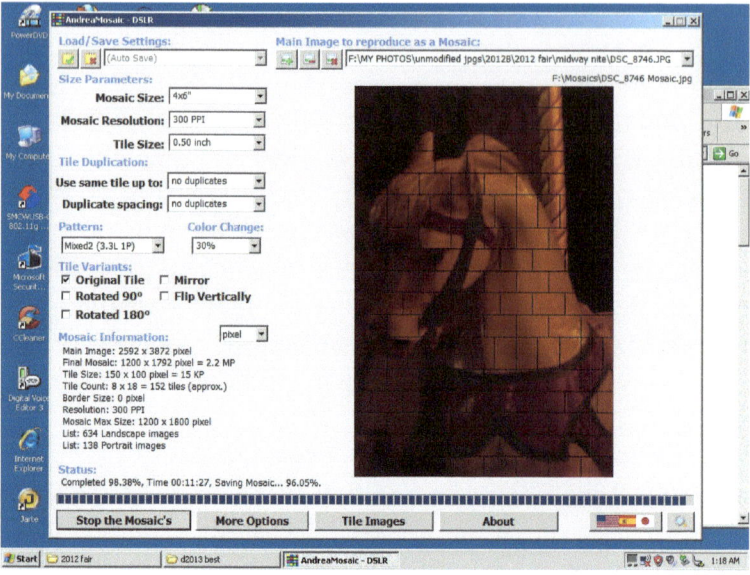

Screen capture of the initial setup for the mosaic

Given the mosaic size, tile size, and tile pattern, the mosaic will use 152 images.

You will also need to set how much color change will be allowed. If you look at the "black" areas in the mosaics that follow, you'll probably wonder how I could have shot them so dark. Answer is, I didn't; I allowed AndreaMosaic to darken them to fit the needs of the mosaic. Some tiles are also considerably bluer than their original images. By default, AndreaMosiac allows a 30% color shift. You probably want to allow more color shifting if your images tend to have similar colors in them (mine images are dominated by might scenes of the midway, so tend to have a lot of black).

Your next decision is whether to allow the program to vary the tiles by rotating of flipping them. This doesn't have as much of an effect as restricting the color change. It depends on how much of a purist you are and how well the landscape/portrait ratio of your images matches the landscape/portrait ratio of the tile pattern. I didn't allow flipping or rotations. (If you see a few landscape orientations that look like they should be portraits, it's because they missed getting oriented when I uploaded them from the cameras.)

If you're using AndreaMosaic for the first time, the mosaic processing will probably be set to "sequential," meaning it takes the tiles in the same order as they are saved in your source folders. If you've allowed the program to freely manipulate the tiles, it might look okay. If you've restricted the ways AndreaMosaic can alter the tiles, it probably won't look like much. Especially if you tend to take several shots of the same subject in sequence.

Which Way Do Carrousels Turn?

Carrousels were the world's first simulators, used in the Middle Ages to practice for a high-pride mounted, circling targeting contest called (what else?) the carrousel (exact spelling varies). Since most people are right-handed, the carrousels turned to the left so the right arm would be able to throw unobstructed. American carrousels still turn left. British carrousels turn right, because they traditionally mount horses from the left.

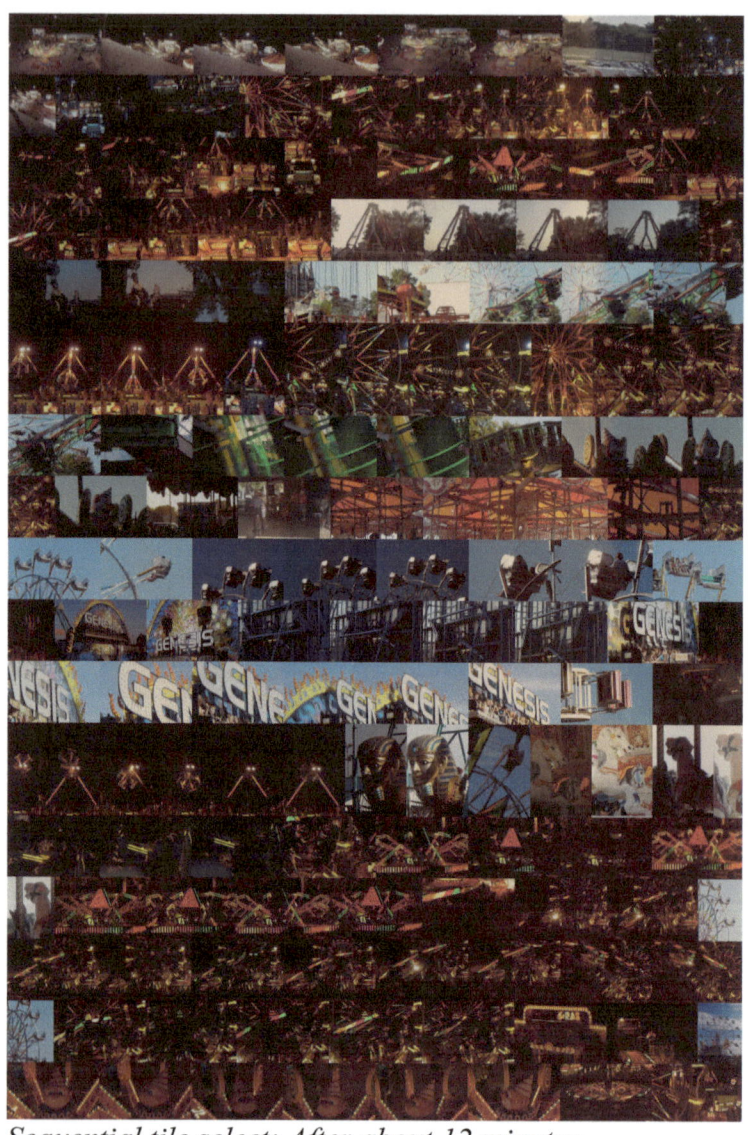

Sequential tile select: After about 12 minutes,
AndreaMosaic presented this. Do you see a horse in this
picture? Me neither.

Well, that was a waste of twelve minutes. Going into the "More Options" menu and changing the tile parameters to "random" at least generates a suggestion of a horse. And adds a little more variety to the tile images.

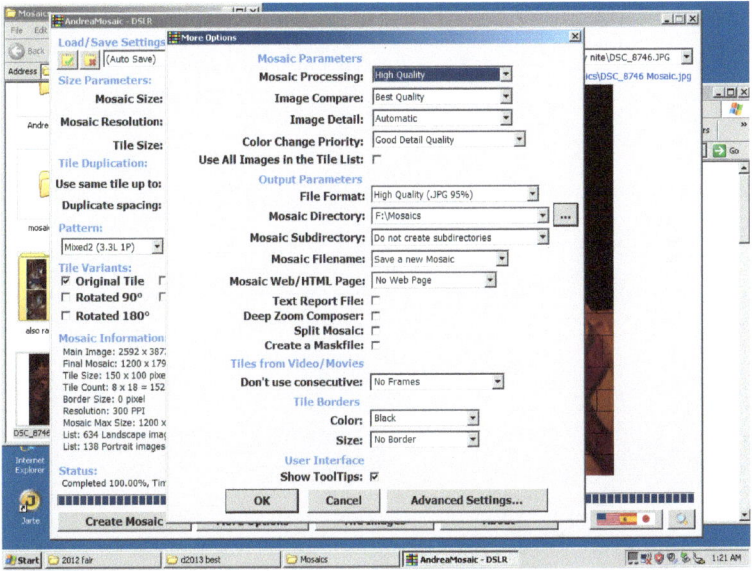

Screen capture of the "More Options" menu.

In the "More Options" menu, we also find we can adjust the priority for the color change. We can lean toward "High Detail" to emphasize the mosaic, or chose "High Quality" to emphasize preserving detail in the individual tiles. Most of these functions can be left alone until we're comfortable with creating a mosaic and want to play around more.

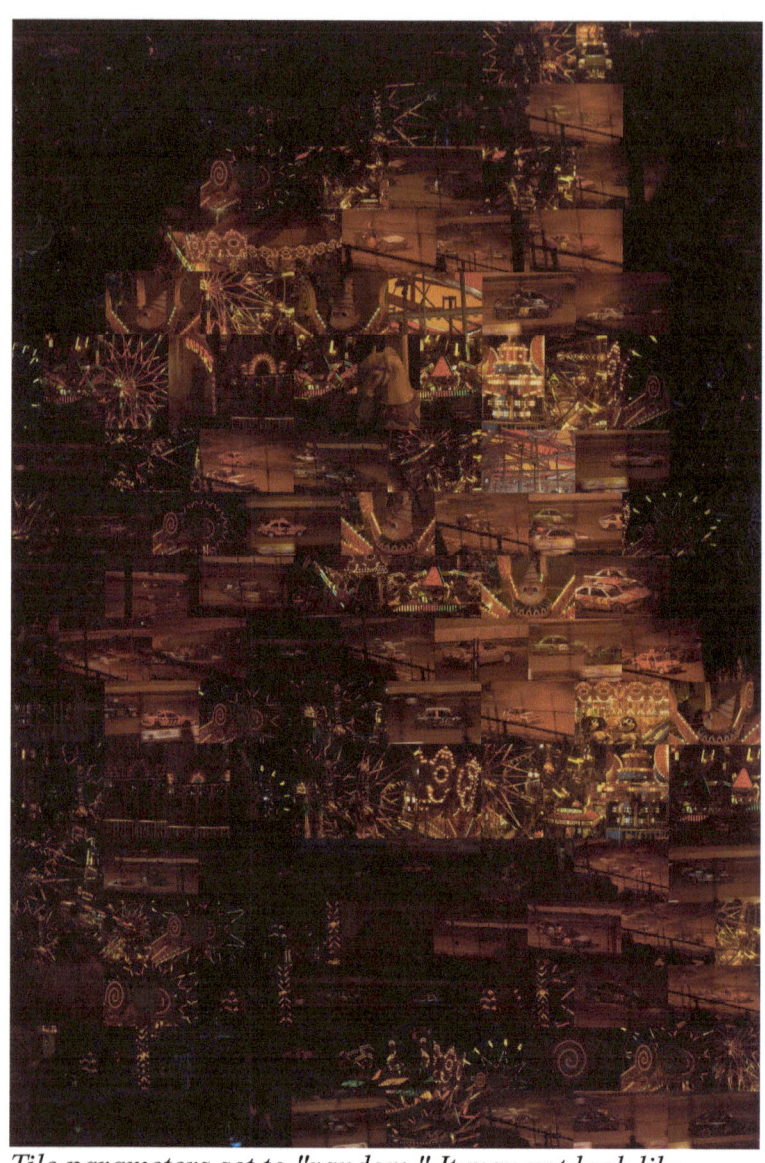

Tile parameters set to "random." It may not look like much at normal reading distance, but viewed at arm's length at least we have the suggestion of a horse.

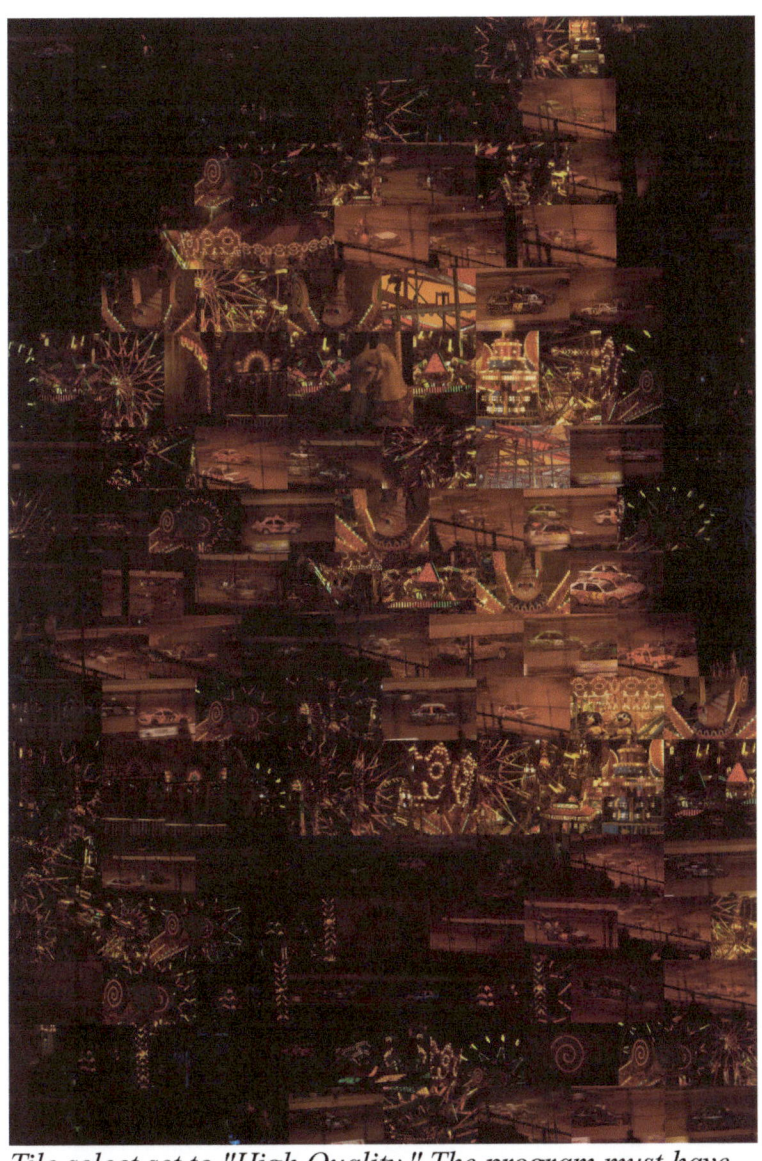

Tile select set to "High Quality." The program must have been happy with the random selection, since it doesn't look any different. But the mosaic overall is muddy.

"High Quality" doesn't seem all that different from "random" (the program must have been satisfied with the random selection). But the image is awfully dark. Let's take it over to the digital darkroom and increase the contrast to bring the horse out of the background.

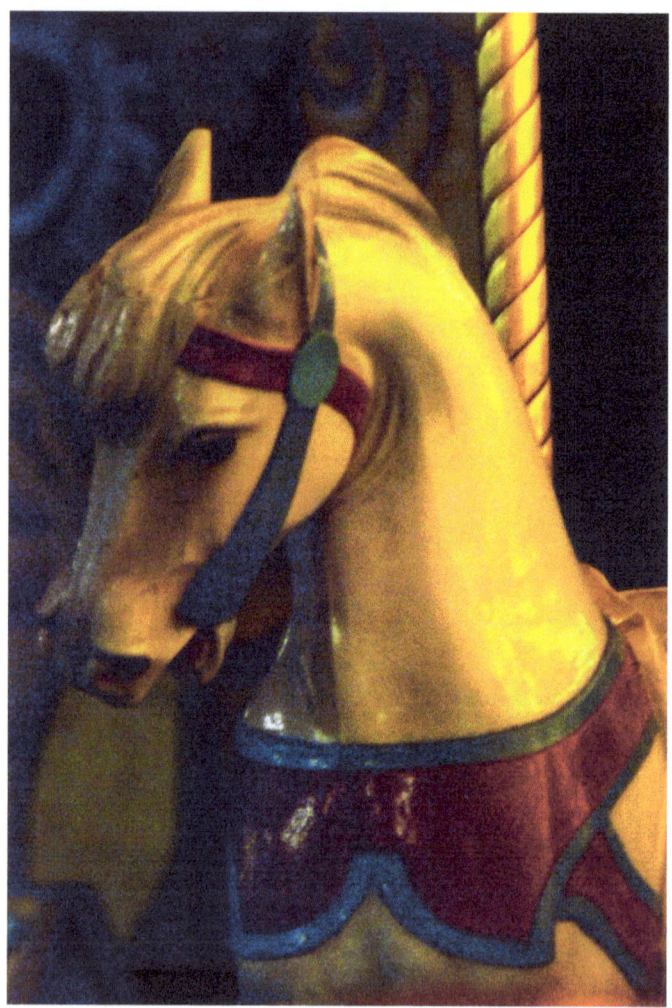

Increasing the contrast helps bring the horse out of the background.

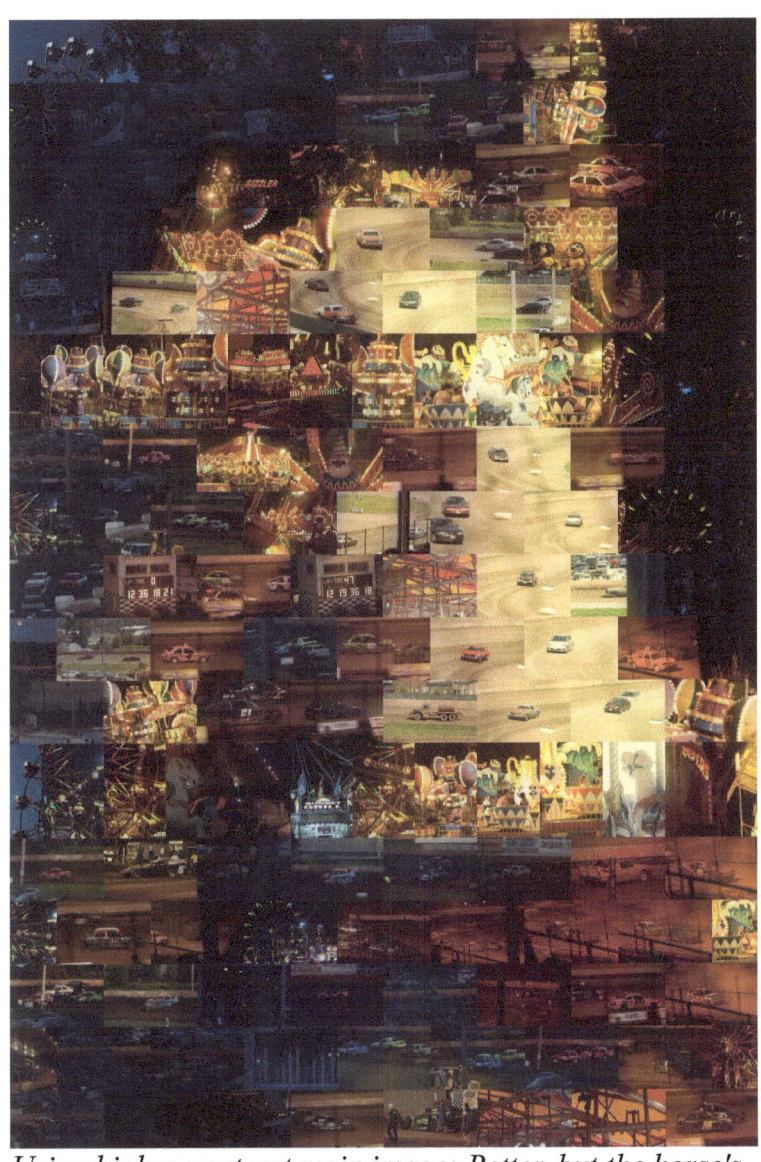

Using higher-contrast main image: Better, but the horse's muzzle is blurring into a bright patch of background.

That's better. It may not look like much up close, but at arm's length, there's definitely a horse there. But a bright patch of background is blending in to the horse's muzzle. Back to the darkroom to burn in the background. While I'm at it, I burn in the other light area near the pole.

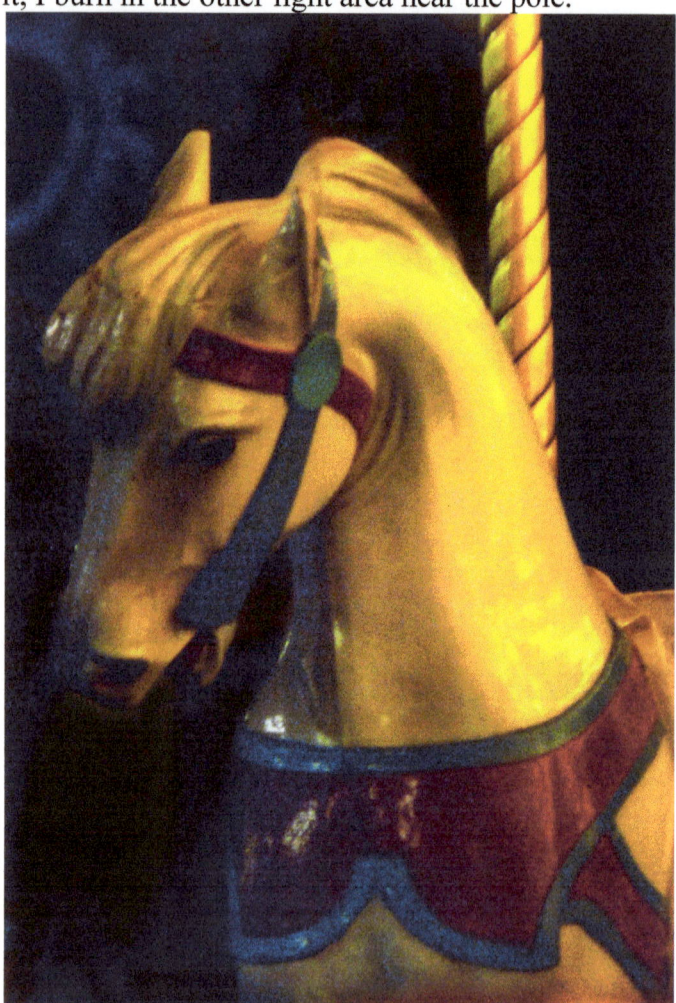

Burning in the area behind the muzzle and pole clarify the horse's contours.

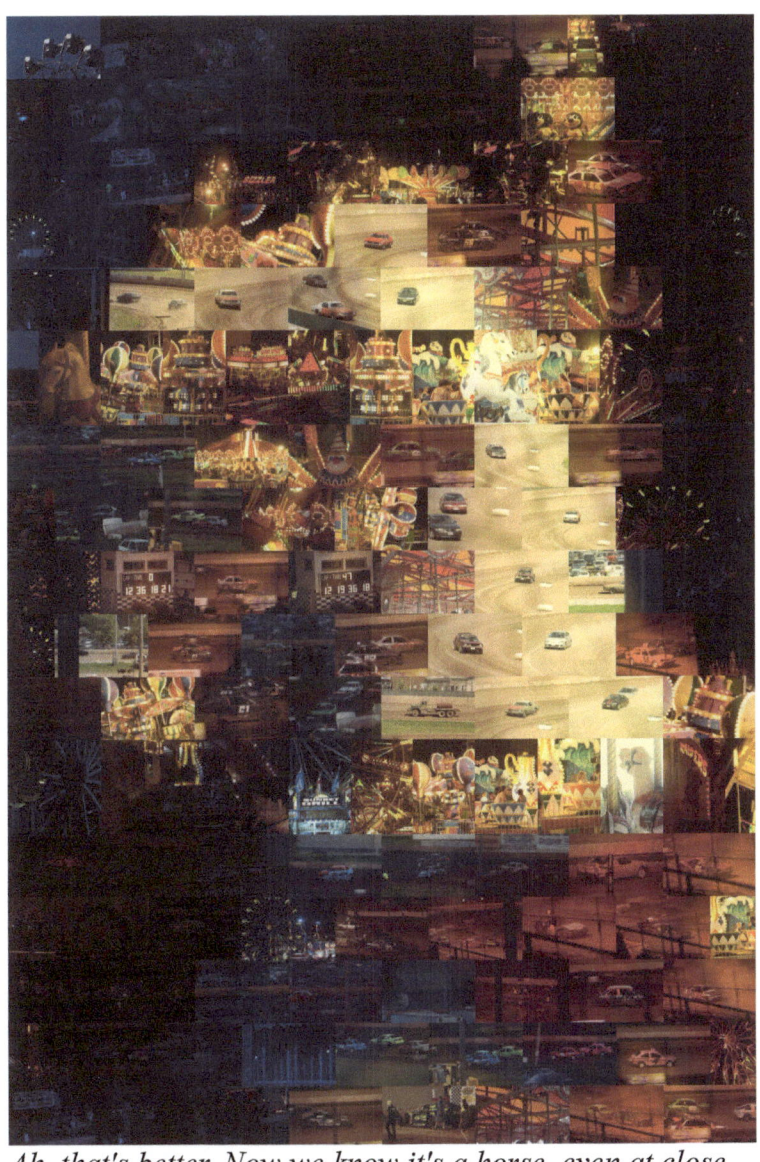

Ah, that's better. Now we know it's a horse, even at close range.

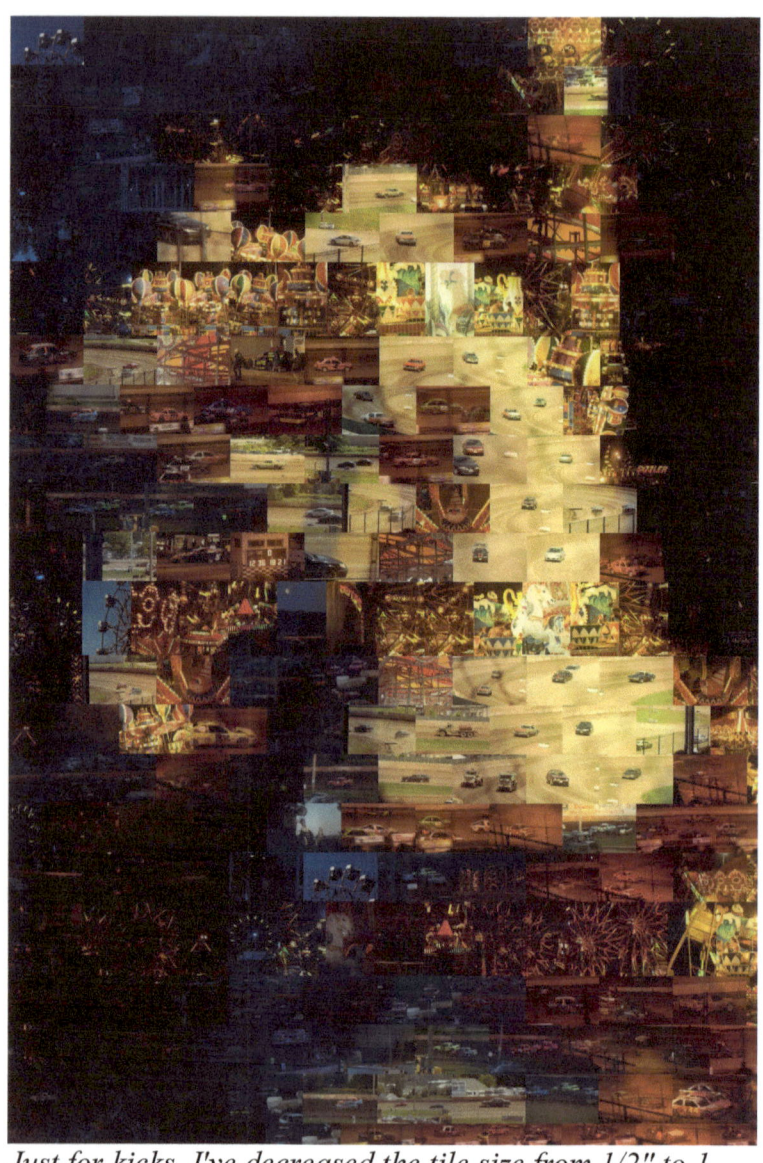

Just for kicks, I've decreased the tile size from 1/2" to 1 cm, resulting in higher detail and more images to show off.

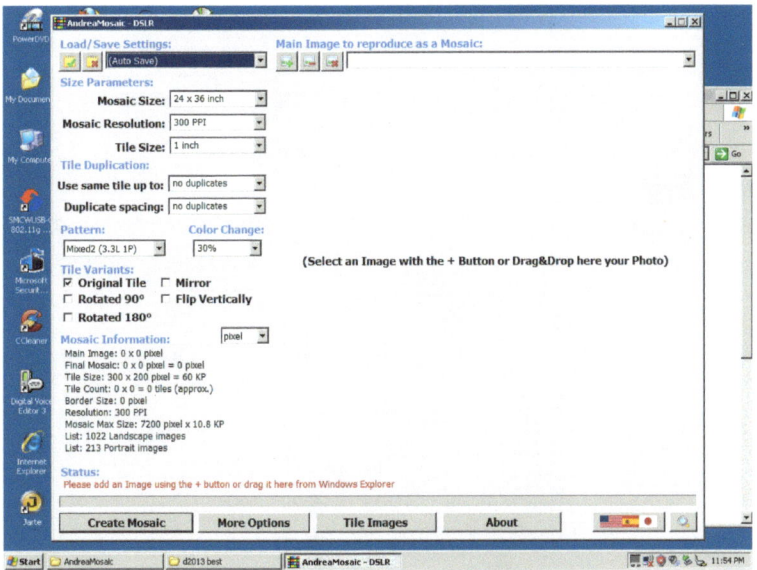

These are the parameters of my "2011 Shawano County Fair" mosaic. The 1233 images were taken over a six-day period requiring daily charges for my brand-new batteries.

My first real use of AndreaMosaic was creating "2011 Shawano County Fair," which took nine attempts (at over two hours each) over the course of three days before I arrived at an acceptable mosaic. The result contained 602 images, all unique. Some of those steps I deliberately recreated for this tutorial, albeit with a much smaller mosaic.

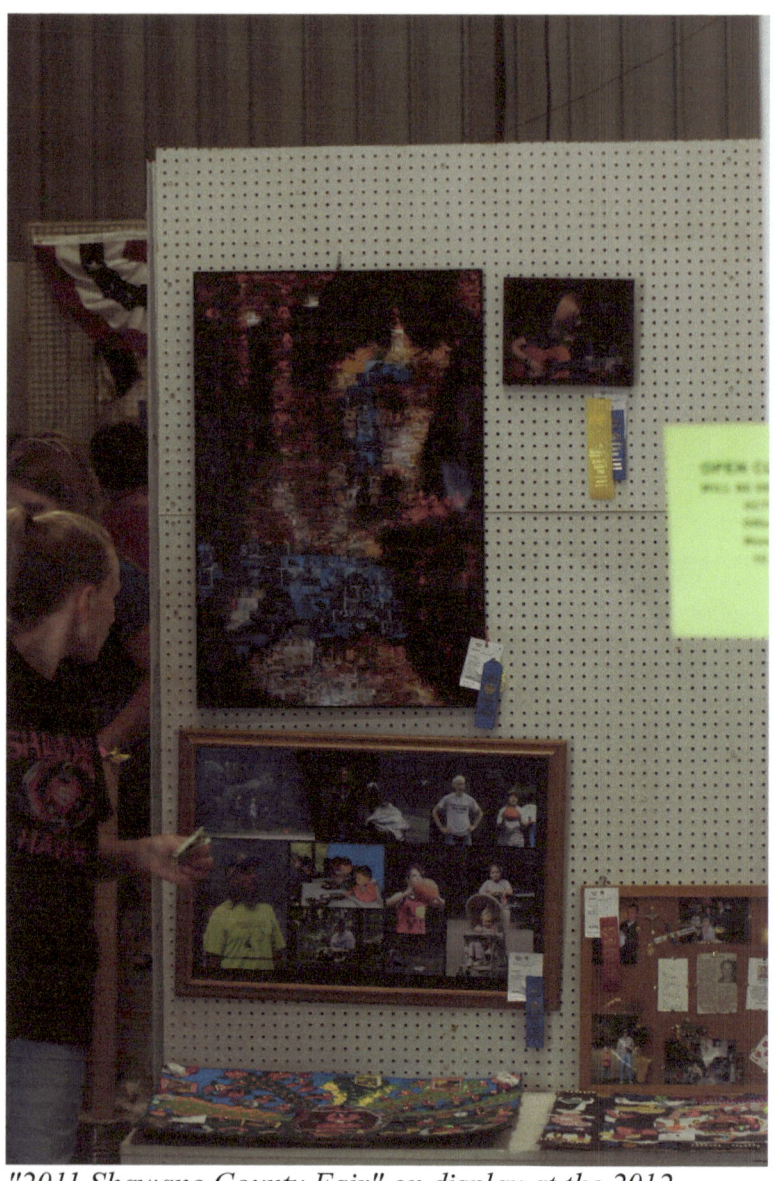

"2011 Shawano County Fair" on display at the 2012 Shawano County Fair.

About This Book

Photos (except page 6) were taken with either a Fuji Finepix Z70, or a Nikon D60 Gold Edition using a 28-70 aspherical Sigma or a 70-210 Quaternary, sometimes with a 2x Vivitar macro-focusing teleconverter.

The photo on page 6 was scanned from an optical print of a negative taken with a Regula IE, a German-made camera which was produced sometime between 1949 and 1953. It is a viewfinder camera, with a 50 mm fixed lens, leaf shutter, and somewhat loose focus, features that make focusing a educated-guessing game and perfectly-focused pictures a complete fluke.

Photo editing was done in Adobe PhotoShop 5.0 LE

Mosaics were created in the free version of AndreaMosiac

The book was written in Open Office 3.4.1.

The creation of this book involved no affiliation with any of them.

www.ingramcontent.com/pod-product-compliance
Lightning Source LLC
Chambersburg PA
CBHW040843180526
45159CB00001B/298